PRIESTLY SPIRITUALITY

GW00771300

HANS URS VON BALTHASAR

PRIESTLY SPIRITUALITY

Translated by Frank Davidson

IGNATIUS PRESS   SAN FRANCISCO

Original German edition:
Priesterliche Spiritualität

© 2007 by Johannes Verlag Einsiedeln, Freiburg

Cover art:
Man of Sorrows
Anonymous, 14th century. Ca. 1370, Italy, Florence
Fresco on canvas
The Cloisters Collection, 1925 (25.120.241)
The Metropolitan Museum of Art, New York
© The Metropolitan Museum of Art/Art Resource, New York

Cover design by Roxanne Mei Lum

© 2013 by Ignatius Press, San Francisco
All rights reserved
ISBN 978-1-58617-693-8
Library of Congress Control Number 2013930749
Printed in the United States of America ∞

CONTENTS

FOREWORD

Priesthood and crisis are two words that appear to be very closely related. Or so it has seemed, at any rate, for the past thirty years and more. The crisis in the priestly ministry is constantly showing new sides, however—the issue of the priest's own self-understanding, for example, the interplay of the various different vocations within the Church, and the struggle, in the face of a plethora of different offices and ministries, to discern what constitutes the specific priestly dimension and identity. Then there is the stress and overload suffered by many priests as a result of the constant structural changes, the sense of having perhaps worked in vain and for nothing, when there is no sign of success—or at any rate of any lasting success—to be seen. Added to this there is the great concern for the future and the problem of awakening new vocations to the priesthood. Are not all these issues inter-related? So, at least, many people rightly ask. The discussion about celibacy as the priestly way of life returns again and again in a series of waves.

7

The question about the nature of the priesthood has been rendered yet more acute by the clear doctrinal statement of the Magisterium that the Church does not have the authority to bestow this ministry upon women. Again and again, in his theological writings, Hans Urs von Balthasar has addressed the fundamental issues of office and ministry, of priesthood and discipleship. In the volumes of his *Skizzen zur Theologie*, especially in *Pneuma und Institution* and also in *Sponsa Verbi*, he has uncovered the foundations from a biblical and theological-historical perspective and has offered answers to the current problems of priestly existence. What he expounded there in broad brushstrokes he has summarized in very concentrated form in a series of shorter essays and articles to be found scattered among various publications. This concentration and density are found here in the present volume. The reader does not linger at the surface but is required to penetrate into the most profound and intimate content of revelation about Christ's work in his Church and about the mission he gave in the sacramental office and the radical nature of what it means to follow him.

Here, what is of enduring validity in the current problem situations is expressed. The reader will observe the confrontation with relevant trends

and at the same time the opposing current gener-
ated by von Balthasar, since he does not follow
popular positions but instead gives us the very
core of the Gospel and of revelation, like rye bread.
It takes perseverance and fidelity to read it,
perhaps—but these are ultimately rewarded by
its nourishing substance. It is reading that invites
us to thoughtful contemplation and deeper reflection. The collection is therefore set out in such a
way that one is not obliged to read the articles
in sequence in order to understand their overall
connection. Instead, one can start anywhere and
will always be led to the center. At the same time
a systematic approach in the structure is revealed and
is perceptible—the center is office, is existence. It
is a teaching not so much about the priesthood as
about priestly existence as such, which takes shape
only in the spirit and in the truth of its origins.
It is fed by the bold presumption of the Lord
in entrusting his mission to weak men and then
strengthening them through his own life of total
self-giving and through the support offered by the
pure figure of the Church in Mary and in her
enduringly fruitful *fiat*. Only when God, made
manifest in the figure of the Savior Jesus Christ,
is understood as the center from which this
priestly existence springs, and only when this

enduring center is proclaimed, can this presumption be understood in confident trust and attract new followers, even in lean times.

Felix Genn
Bishop of Essen

INTRODUCTION TO THE TEXTS

The essays and articles by Hans Urs von Balthasar on priestly spirituality that have been gathered together in this volume form neither a unified nor an exhaustive treatise but are instead a collection of texts written on different occasions and for different reasons. Nevertheless, the unity underlying them is revealed in the understanding of priestly spirituality. How is this to be characterized? What features does he emphasize?

In order to illuminate the life of the priest of today, von Balthasar goes back to the origins, to the apostles, to their calling, to their wanderings with Jesus along the roads of Galilee in Judaea, and above all to that moment from which their apostolic mission and their entire Christian existence originates, namely, the Paschal mystery of Jesus. On the eve of his death, Jesus establishes the Eucharist and the priesthood; immediately after his Resurrection he bestows on the disciples the power to forgive sins, entrusts his sheep to Peter, and sends all eleven of them out into the whole world. Thus von Balthasar considers the life and mission of today's shepherds in continuity not only with the first apostles but above all with Jesus himself. The person and mission of Jesus Christ stand at the center of priestly spirituality. Hence all the reflections in the texts that follow revolve unswervingly around Jesus Christ and his mission. Jesus is the source and norm of priestly existence.

The priestly office signifies the power to exercise authority for the good of the community. This authority comes, not "from below", from men, but "from above", from God, from Christ. No one can appropriate this authority to himself; no one has a right to it. Mission always comes from God. And for this mission God demands the whole person. The one who is called relinquishes, completely, his own self, his private life. Everything is given for the sake of the mission, which is one of service for the People of God. God expects of the one called that he will place himself wholly at his disposal, in faith, in obedience, and in inner self-abandonment; that he will entrust himself unreservedly to the guidance of God. The awareness of having been called by God and the identification with the mission thereby accepted form the identity of the one who has "left everything".

It belongs to the task of the shepherd not only to transmit the message authentically and with authority, but also to live it. The shepherds must be "examples to the flock" (1 Pet 5:3). This is possible only if the existence of the one proclaiming is in harmony with the Word proclaimed. Von Balthasar returns again and again to this unity between the objective authority, derived from the sacrament of Holy Orders, and the personal, existential commitment of the priest. The priesthood is a matter, not of a profession, but of participation in the redemptive work of Christ, a personal and existential participation that will cost the individual concerned his entire personal life. The priest must engage in his mission with his whole person. The authority to act in the name of Christ is unthinkable except in living communion with Jesus. "In the New Covenant there can be no 'office' that is not existentially 'covered'", von Balthasar writes. For Jesus himself represents the perfect combination of mission and person. "Jesus Christ is purely and simply the identity of office and existence, the mission personified." In his redemptive suffering he is at once Priest and Victim; he is the one officiating and the one who suffers to the ultimate degree. Jesus is the executor of the priestly office only to the degree that he experiences himself, existentially, as a Victim offered to God. If the authority of the priestly office is to endure in his Church, then it can only be in close association with the existential form of total self-emptying and self-offering. The priesthood of the New Testament is participation in the identity of Priest and Victim.

"Since in Christ office and life have become identical . . . for a Christian office bearer the highest possible degree of convergence is not merely appropriate but an absolute requirement." In saying this it is impossible to overlook the fact that the priesthood of Jesus, in the unity of office and person, is fully revealed and realized precisely in his self-offering on the Cross. "The New Covenant is actually established only with the slaughter of the new *Pascha*—in the night of the Cross. . . . It is precisely here, in the night of the Cross, that the New Testament priestly office originates." Only the one who truly loves can reach this place (the Cross). Love is the sole power that holds the priest firmly there where he should stand. And where should he stand? Where is the proper place of the priest? In the Cenacle, at the washing of feet; on the Mount of Olives; beneath the Cross. To be a priest of the New Testament means humbly to take upon oneself the filth of others, not merely to offer to God in reparation the blood—the alien blood—of animals, but "to be crucified with Christ" (Gal 2:19) in imitation of Christ. To be in union with Christ in his life and death is the only valid starting point for the ministry of the priestly office. Even before they assume this office, the twelve future apostles are already called upon to follow Christ personally; they are initiated existentially into the mystery of the Cross. Even though the actual moment of the Cross will only come later for the disciples ("but when you are old . . ."), it must be clear, right from the very beginning, that to follow Christ means to "renounce everything". Already, at the first meeting of the disciples with Jesus, this is precisely the issue; they must leave everything, stake everything on this one card, to follow Jesus unconditionally. This "leaving everything" is moreover not merely the first, indispensable step; rather, it must become a permanent attitude and way of life if the path of imitation is to be a successful one. It becomes the foundation of the attitude that will later be expressed in the concept of the "evangelical counsels". The evangelical radicalism demanded of the priest—whom the Church enjoins to celibacy—brings the priesthood to a state close to that of these counsels. Through the sacrament of Holy Orders, a man is not only consecrated for the service of God within the Church; he also becomes a part of the presbyterium. This can be lived out in practice in a variety of different priestly associations. A priestly community is not merely a given fact that must be respected ("and he called the Twelve to himself . . ."—as a community, and not as an assemblage of individuals), but also a practical existential aid, especially when the priest is required to work in a situation where he suffers as a solitary individual. The mission in an unbelieving world presupposes the background of a community of brothers.

Selflessness, evangelical counsels, following Christ on the way to Jerusalem—all these things presuppose and simultaneously nurture an important virtue for the one called to be a leader in the Church, namely, humility. Jesus humbled himself in his priesthood and "became obedient unto death" (Phil 2:8); on behalf of sinners he took upon himself the most extreme humiliation. That is why Peter, before receiving his office, is humbled by the question about love—the love that he has denied—and given the promise that he will follow Christ to the Cross— against his will ("where you would rather not go").

The ministry of the priest is a ministry of authority. Jesus has freed us from obedience to the Law and given us the freedom of the children of God, and yet he has given his Church this ministry of authority, "because he has freed the world from the disobedience of sin through his obedience to the Father". Jesus, who enjoined the disciples to obedience as only

God himself can do, was the first to prove himself in obedience. To be a bearer of authority and to enjoin others to obedience in the name of Christ signifies—according to von Balthasar—a mortification (the first must become the last) and demands a radical humility without which the sinner will be unable to fight against the temptation to abuse power. This ministry is likewise a humiliation because those who hold it must experience again and again the insuperable tension between the helplessness of man and the power of God that has been granted to his Church, the tension between their own individual dissimilarity to Christ and a genuine official representation of the Person of Christ. This tension—this paradox of power in weakness—is one that can only be endured in faith. Faith and humility enable the priest to convey objective certainty, to present the Word of God simply and with perseverance, to dispense sacramental grace and sanctify the faithful—not by the power of his own holiness but by the power of God's holiness. A humble priest will never represent himself as an example, even though he knows that it is his duty to be an example to the flock. Nor will he ever regard his own limitations and weakness as a restriction of the power of divine action.

Although the priest knows that his own holiness can never measure up to the magnitude of his mission, the requirement nonetheless remains for him to bring his personal life into harmony with what his office represents. The office of Christ can be genuinely exercised only in the spirit of Christ. Hence Peter is entrusted with his office only after professing his love. However, the priest may trust— conscious of his own personal inadequacy—in the power of the Communion of Saints, in the "Johannine" love, the love that "sustains" the Church of Peter, but also and above all in the holiness of the Church herself, in the Immaculate One, in the Mother of the Church.

The spirituality of the priest is necessarily ecclesial and Marian. A servant of the Church cannot bypass the Virgin Mary, for "the actual and original image of the Church is Mary, not Peter, who will only exercise a function within the Church." Mary stands in a very close relationship to the priesthood. On the one hand, what actually constitutes the true meaning of the priesthood, namely, service of the Church, has already happened decisively in the Virgin Mary. Through her Yes to the Word of God, she has made possible his Incarnation. Christ gives life to the world, and through this life, his Life, the Church, his Body, lives. Mary received it beneath the Cross—on behalf of us all (just as she had already conceived the Word, in the name of us all, at the moment of the

Annunciation)—and now his life becomes "Body" in humanity, in the Church. Mary is the Mother of the Church, she is "Co-Origin of the Church". But she also plays a role in another event, one that is crucially important for the priesthood, namely, the Eucharistic Sacrifice. The sacrifice of Christ that is made present in the Eucharist is above all the sacrifice of Jesus, but at the same time it is a sacrifice of the Mother, who, along with him, offers up her Son. Hence it is also the sacrifice of the Mother-Church. All the fruitfulness of the priest is ultimately the fruitfulness of the Mother-Church; the validity of his office springs not from his personal perfection but from the perfection of the Immaculate Mother. In this respect, a priest becomes a worthwhile instrument of the power of God, and his priestly life becomes fruitful, only to the extent that he immerses himself and, indeed, "disappears" in the Mystery of the love between the Bridegroom Christ and his Bride the Church.

Vojtěch Brož

ON PRIESTLY SPIRITUALITY

Whoever begins to reflect on this topic—and what priest or candidate for the priesthood could fail to do so?—must first of all take into consideration the relative and problematical aspects of the word spirituality. For Christians there is ultimately only one kind—the demonstration of loving and hope-filled faith or the observance to the great double commandment. In any case, the manner in which this can occur in the various "states" and "offices" of the Church is a secondary matter. If we make this a primary issue, then different spiritualities can be set against each other and played off against each other as though they were closed and even self-sufficient entities, rather than organs of a single living organism; organs that possess their specific function solely in the interests of unity and as distinctive aspects of it and that are kept alive only through the circulating lifeblood that flows through and is common to them all.

On the other hand, according to the detailed teaching of Saint Paul, there truly is a differentiation

among the organs—and specifically, as he emphasizes, for the sake of unity and for the sake of its
living vitality; hence it would be equally mistaken
to seek to "level out" the special nature of these
functions within the overall unity, simply because
all live the same faith and the same great commandment. An example of such leveling, in this
case, would be if one were to place the various
offices—which according to Paul are expressly "measured out" to the individual by God (Rom 12:3c) and
by Christ (Eph 4:11)—as though they were somehow assigned as something indifferent in the disposal of the Church, so that she could arbitrarily
allocate these (essential) offices and withdraw them
again, rather as the state assigns and reshuffles positions. The fact that there are indeed essential offices
that are crucial to the basic structure of the Church
is evident from the entire New Testament, and hence
it is also clear that the Church cannot simply remodel
her basic structure through some kind of theological gene manipulation.

How, then, can we find a way through, between
these two apparently opposing elementary princi-
ples, to a proper and neither overheated nor under-
valued spirituality of the priesthood? One practical
pointer for the approach to be taken might perhaps
be found in the problem, which has only recently

become such a burning issue, of the demand by many women to share in the priestly office. Indeed, if it were the case that an incomparable dignity and close-ness to Christ lay in the priestly office, if we were to see in it in some sense the summit of perfection, how then could the female sex be fundamentally excluded from it? We recall the historical line of rea-soning, originating with Dionysius the Areopagite and received by Thomas Aquinas, which so closely linked the bishop and the *status perfectionis acquisi-tae*, and its dubious aftermath in the theory of Cardinal Mercier that the sole "order", or state of perfection, founded by Christ was the diocesan clergy with the bishop at their head. If one were to accept this uncritically, would not the revolution of women (in America in particular, but also in Europe) then be entirely understandable?

One might recommend starting at the very point in the Gospels where this supposed "order" was founded. Viewing the matter objectively, it is clear that it is not the first concern of Jesus to establish and develop in detail an ecclesial organism in order to substitute it for the old constitution of Israel. Indeed, he does not even begin with external struc-tures; rather, he begins with radical internal demands in which the "spirituality" of Israel must fulfill itself, since the conversion of the Chosen People would necessarily have been of foremost importance. It was impossible that the Messiah, whom the people were awaiting in accordance with his most intensive promises, should not have begun his work first of all as the one who fulfills the entire salvation history of the People of God, in order then—just as necessarily and in accordance with these same promises—to complete the transition to what is universal, the "Light to enlighten the Gentiles" (Lk 2:32). The first articulations of what is new, the first fulfillments, are found in the call to radical discipleship, to unconditional accompaniment: the call to leave everything (Mk 1:17, 20; 2:14; Lk 5:11; Mt 19:27), to impose no limiting conditions (Mt 8:16–22 par), to stake everything on the one card—initially as a quite literal "following after Jesus", without knowing in advance where this will lead (Jn 1:39). What the first disciples are engaged in here is a resolute, even if surely not fully thought-out, obedient consent to the instruction given by Jesus. It is something along the lines of the perfect *fiat* of the "handmaid of the Lord", through whom the Incarnation of the Word of God was made possible and came about. Had she attached conditions to her Yes, then obstacles would have been raised that would have prevented God's Word from entering the medium of the human in order to nourish itself therefrom as a child is nurtured from his mother. In the unconditional Yes of Mary, the faith of Abraham is perfected; also perfected is the covenant on Mount Sinai, and the New and Eternal Covenant prophesied by Jeremiah becomes reality—the Word is truly placed in the heart of the Mother (cf. Jer 31:31, 33). For the first time the response is adequate, whereby the teleology of the Old Covenant has been fulfilled in the New and the synagogue has essentially become the Church, the *Ecclesia immaculata* (Eph 5:27). It is a concrete Yes, incarnated in the spiritual-physical heart of Mary in which the Incarnation of the Word is accomplished. So, too, the Yes of the disciples, who leave everything, is first of all a literal following, as befits the word-form of the call given by Jesus. Only from this point onward is it permissible and justifiable to apply a "spiritual" and more generalized interpretation (as is found above all with Luke and Paul)—even those who possess worldly goods must in spirit leave everything behind; even the man who is married to a wife and knows the works and workings of *eros* must live in spirit "as though he were not married", must wherever possible make *eros* into an expression of *agape*. So too those who acquire things—in other words, those who possess earthly goods—should be as though they possessed nothing, in other words, as though they had placed all their goods at the service of the Lord.

Of course Jesus is not establishing any "order" (such a thing will only later find its organic place within an already established Church). But we can indeed say that the first and fundamental thing, which he both establishes and insists upon, is that radical deed and outlook that were later described with the (perhaps misleading) expression "evangelical counsels", namely, the perfect, obedient willingness to follow him wherever he goes—even there where there is no longer a place to lay one's head—a total self-emptying, since he "became poor, so that by his poverty you might become rich" (2 Cor 8:9). It means being totally available for the cause of the Kingdom; in other words, celibacy, as Jesus lives it, in order to be able to dispense himself in his entirety, eucharistically fruitful, to his own and, indeed, to the world.

If this is the underlying stratum upon which everything else rests, then two things follow from it. First, the fact that women (in Mary) share just as much in the essentials as men (in the discipleship of the first disciples, who will later receive and exercise the priestly ministry); indeed, women are even more favored here, since Mary's *fiat* is inimitably perfect, whereas that of the disciples, as the Gospels reveal, will prove to be deficient in many ways. And so the actual and original image *of* the

14 -12 ffi   love fonto
   priests

Church is Mary, not Peter, who will only exercise a function *within* the Church. The second point, however, is this: the fundamental basis of all priestly spirituality—whether it concerns the religious or the secular clergy—must lie in that radical and "literal" discipleship which was later characterized as the "evangelical counsels" but also known in the Middle Ages as the *vita apostolica.*[1] An eloquent proof of this is found in the numerous encyclicals of recent popes concerning priestly perfection, which, strikingly, is always described according to the schema of the evangelical counsels, albeit with an emphasis on the unique character of the priesthood.[2] Accordingly, the Bishops' Synod of 1971 spoke, especially in relation to the celibacy of the priest, not only of a *plena concordantia* but of an *intima cohaerentia*, "which excludes the perception of priestly virginity as merely a particular and limited charism, given only to a few, which could accordingly be easily unwoven from the fabric of the priestly vocation".

Of course, only the foundation is thereby laid upon which the particular character of the priestly

---

[1] On this general issue, see my work *Christlicher Stand* (Einsiedeln: Johannesverlag, 1977); translated by Mary Frances McCarthy as *The Christian State of Life* (San Francisco: Ignatius Press, 1983).

[2] Ibid., 255–59; English ed., 315–21.

ministry is established. Yet it is established in such a way that it always presupposes this foundation—indeed its every particularity is inextricably mixed with this constitutive foundation. Precisely because the priest will be called to the distinctive role of "pastor" of the community, he must participate in a particular and indeed visible manner—corresponding to the visible character of the Church—in the constitutive structure of the community as a whole.

Let us look back once more at the stages in the life of Jesus. The first calling, to "leave everything" and follow him, aims at gaining helpers for the work of the conversion of Israel. To fulfill this work, the Twelve are initially given powers analogous to those of Jesus—for preaching the Kingdom and effectively repressing the sphere of activity of the evil spirits (Mk 3:14–15). As to the priestly power to preside at the Eucharistic celebration and to forgive sins, we cannot yet logically speak of this except in immediate association with the Passion, since the Eucharist is instituted only "on the day before he suffered" and the sacrament of Penance "on the day after he suffered", at Easter (Jn 20:23).[3]

---

[3] The now increasingly accepted view that Matthew 16:18f. (and, correspondingly, also 18:18, in the "community" chapter) of Matthew has been predated and in fact belongs—as in John 21—in the time after the Resurrection, may well be the right one.

Perhaps (together with A. Feuillet)[4] we may see in John 17:19 a hint that what is really being spoken of here is priestly ordination as a sacrament (which indeed is closely connected in practice with the Eucharistic event, cf. 1 Cor 11:24c). What is central, however, is the scene between the risen Lord and Peter (Jn 21:15–19). Though already long since chosen to be the spokesman, he is now expressly entrusted with the office of pastor, along with the demand for the highest degree of love ("more than these others?" verse 15) and the promise of conformity with him in the crucifixion (verse 19), whereby the demand and the promise refer to each other. Because the newly appointed shepherd must now follow Christ in his pastoral ministry, he must be willing to make the same total commitment of his life (even to the cross). Moreover, he must do so in imitation of the Good Shepherd, out of a "greater love" (and not merely out of a sense of conscientious official duty), so that at least in the first pastor of the Church it is possible also to imitate the pastoral ministry of Christ.

So we find ourselves plunged into the very heart of the description of priestly spirituality, for we must assume that Peter is not to be seen here (in a

[4] *Le Sacerdoce du Christ et de ses ministres* (Paris: Ed de Paris, 1971).

Protestant sense) as a unique exception but rather as a "type" of all his "co-elders" (1 Pet 5:1, 3) who themselves thereby have to become "types of the flock". A glance at Paul, who sets forth in the greatest detail the unity of his ministry and his evangelical existence in word and deed, demonstrates this irrefutably. This central element is so clear that it requires no further elucidation.

The point to which everything comes down is this: the total self-giving to Christ (leaving everything, even wife and child: Lk 18:30) is now wedded to the task of committing this totality to the service of the flock of Christ and finds in this its practical application. Also, this entire service, in the Catholic understanding, is not like any worldly "job" but is a special kind of participation in the redemptive work of the Son—who was obedient unto death—and is thus itself marked by this work. The words of Saint Paul: "I rejoice in my sufferings . . . and in my flesh [that is, my entire earthly existence] complete what is lacking in Christ's afflictions for the sake of his body, that is, the Church" (Col 1:24), do not of course mean that the sufferings of Christ were inadequate but, rather, that he has reserved a place in his all-sufficient sufferings for us to suffer with him in "com-passion". First of all, for his Mother, of course, who is the archetype of the Church, but then also for the official servants of the Church (like Peter and Paul), who in their entire existence of service are allowed, together with the Master, to wear themselves out for the sake of his body, the Church—and how often seemingly in vain, just as the work of Jesus as a whole was also seemingly in vain.

This total commitment of the priest, which demands and devours his life as a whole, distinguishes him from all those other forms of partial commitment which—however deep—still have other irons in the fire in addition to this pastoral ministry—whether it be in a marriage or in other kinds of professional occupation. Twenty pastoral assistants together do not make up one priest. It is a deceptive illusion to argue that some certain number of partial functions performed by the priest could in fact equally be taken over by laymen or deacons. Why stop at this division and then reserve the two remaining functions of eucharistic consecration and sacramental absolution to the priest alone and then, on top of that, demand of him a celibate existence? This is therefore a—often maliciously—manufactured illusion, since the singling out of these partial and subsidiary functions always presupposes the organic unity of the overall competence; the auxiliary function presupposes the central function that it assists. A glance

at the New Testament from the time of the first community (Acts 1:15ff.) through to the post-Pauline
times (cf. Tit 1:5), and still more in the subsequent
centuries of the history of the Church, demonstrates this unequivocally. No amount of ecumenical leveling will deprive the Catholic people of their
healthy instinct in this respect. Not merely in regard
to the central unity of this ministry—in the parish
as in the diocese, I would imagine—but also in regard
to the requirement of a celibate existence for the sake
of the community as this concrete part of the Body
of Christ. The widespread expectation of a trans-
formation of lay theologians into *viri probati* will
unexpectedly encounter strong resistance in the par-
ishes and will no doubt provoke a hitherto unknown
turning to the remaining religious clergy.

To return once more from here to the starting
theme, if the evangelical requirement to renounce
everything was seen there as the foundation of all
that followed, it was not in any way in order to
revive the outdated medieval debate. There is no
question of blurring the distinction between what
has emerged within the Church as the "religious
state" and the hierarchically ordered priesthood. The
former, to which both women and men belong, has
to a large extent assumed specific forms that in their
details in no way need to be applied to priests. And

the life of the ministerial priesthood has, as we have shown, its own particular demands that are not included in the general call to follow Christ. No sheep, however gifted, can as such assume the functions of the shepherd. Instead there are two things that remain: first, the requirement of evangelical radicalism on the part of the pastors of the Church—which in practice includes celibacy—and, secondly, certain forms of rapprochement between priesthood and the evangelical counsels, such as exist in the many different kinds of priestly associations with their particular obligations, rules, and so on—mostly to the great advantage of the priests themselves. Among the most important aspects of such associations is the experience of a genuine and effective communion, even if the individual pastors have to live singly. Such experience of communion, together with the possibility of mutual support in the loneliness of the modern secularized environment, is for a great many, and perhaps for almost all of them, an indispensable requirement. The Christian existence is always lived mysteriously between ecclesial communion and the witness of missionary solitude—each has to confess his faith, exposed to the unbelieving world. In this exposed solitude he must be conscious of the community *behind him*—just as the Twelve were conscious, as they spread out in every direction, of their belonging to the College. Priestly associations perform this service today, giving the isolated priest the awareness of concrete ecclesiastical communion that neither the parish nor the diocese is capable of providing him in sufficiently tangible form.

MARY AND THE OFFICE
OF THE PRIEST

It is not easy to speak about Mary. One is conscious
from Church history of the overstepping of bound-
aries both to the right and to the left—on the one
hand, such exalted praises that her status is almost,
if not altogether, equated with that of her Son:
"Everything that applies to the Son applies likewise
to the Mother" was an assertion made by certain
mediaeval theologians. To Mary was attributed the
power to persuade her Son at the Judgment and
even—according to a well-known legend—to res-
cue souls already condemned to hell, and so on.
Then, on the other hand, there is such understatement that sees in Mary nothing more than an especially outstanding member of the Church, which
is—according to an isolated but much quoted com-
ment of Saint Augustine—as far above her as the
whole is over the part. One can hardly deny that even
the Second Vatican Council, in its beautiful Marian chapter at the end of the Dogmatic Constitution on the Church, likewise suffers a little from such

understatement, for fear of falling back into the over-heated theory of privileges. It does not seem to be easy for men, who indeed see themselves above all as the master builders of theology, to describe the unique position, not only of women in general, but of this Woman in particular. The history of Mariology is in many respects such a history of excesses and recessions.

In seeking to strike the right tone, we will endeavor to avoid all sentimentality but also all resentment and to hold soberly to the solid facts of revelation, while nonetheless seeing these facts for what they are, namely, as events involving persons of "real-symbolic" [*realsymbolisch*—efficacious or "sacramental"] significance. In the trinitarian self-revelation of God, everything is the work of persons, of course—in other words, nothing is abstract—yet these persons have a general, "catholic" significance—and the more so the more closely they are associated with the catholic Person of Jesus Christ, in whom God makes himself known, with transcendent validity, to all men "from every nation, from all tribes and peoples and tongues" (Rev 7:9).

Two persons stand out particularly in the New Testament: Mary, in whose *fiat* the entire faith of the Old Covenant comes to maturity, in preparation for the reception of the final promise and fulfillment of

God—mentioned again and again at such decisive moments in the life of Jesus until finally delivered in the culminating event of the Cross and from there released into the Church; and Peter, upon whom, as the foundation stone, this visible Church is established, with the promise of invincibility in the face of the powers of darkness and the bestowal of an authority that—issuing from heaven—binds this same heaven to the decisions of earthly-ecclesial authority. Both these persons are recipients of missions that go far beyond the private sphere; both stand in the closest possible relationship to the Catholic Church as a whole. Hence, the question is: Do they meet? Do their spheres touch, penetrate each other? Is there perhaps a need for a mediating figure in order to make explicit their unity in the one Church of Christ?

And so, in a first section we will examine the "real-symbol" that is Mary, and in a second section the "real-symbol" that is Peter (who will here represent especially the foundation of the priesthood). Then, in a third section, we will deal with the mediation of the two within the unity of the *catholica*.

1. Mary-Church

When John uses the phrase "And the Word became flesh" (by flesh he means mortal man), he is thereby expressing the transition from the Old Covenant, with a Chosen People, to a New Covenant that embraces "every nation . . . all tribes and peoples and tongues", addressed to and including all that is flesh and human. We must take this expression so seriously as to recognize that the entire humanity of Jesus—his speech and his silences, his rejoicing and tears, his anger and zeal and his weariness, even his exasperation at remaining among men—is an expression of the inner mind of God, a mind that already in the Old Covenant was depicted in largely "anthropomorphic" terms. We have to understand that the Word of God truly assumes the *morphé anthrópou*, the form, or likeness, of man (cf. Phil 2:7), in order to be "seen, heard, and touched" as it is. We need only observe, in saying this, that what Jesus says and does and presents is always the transmission of what he is meant to represent: "My teaching is not mine, but his who sent me" (cf. Jn 7:16). In this existence of Jesus—who in his totality is the representation, the articulation of the universal God—is rooted in what we call ecclesial "real symbol".

First of all Mary. In the scene of the Annunciation, when she speaks the Yes of the handmaid to this Incarnation of the Word, then this Yes cannot be a private event but must instead be spoken, as Thomas Aquinas says, "on behalf of the entire human race"—in other words, as the fulfillment of the faith-filled assent of Abraham to the covenant that God made with him, in which however, all the nations of the earth were, in prospect, to be blessed (Gen 12:3). As a result—as Paul never tires of declaring—from the start, the faith of Israel looked forward, beyond the national covenant, and included in itself the salvation even of the heathens, of Assyria, and of Egypt (Is 19:23f.; Jer 12:14f.). Thus the Yes of Mary must be universal, from both perspectives: from the origin in Abraham—which leaves room for all the as yet unforeseeable promises of God—and still more so from the end of the promise, from the Incarnation of the Word, since Mary has to assent fully to the limitless fate of her Son, whom she will have to accompany as a Mother along his entire path, wherever this path may lead.

Note that in the Annunciation by the angel two things are made evident (both together constituting the exact fulfillment of God's covenant with Abraham and Moses), namely, the absolute sovereignty of God, who alone determines the fact and the content of the covenant, and then the consideration for the partner to this covenant, the creature of God endowed with freedom, whose freedom is not overwhelmed but instead respected and who must therefore express his assent to the terms of the covenant. The sovereignty of God finds expression in the fact that God does not make his action conditional upon the decision of the creature but speaks already in the future tense: you *will* conceive and bear a son; you *shall* call his name Jesus. He *will* be Son of the Most High and *will* reign over the house of Jacob. And yet this event is announced to the "handmaid of the Lord", who is addressed as "full of grace"; her Yes is an essential part of the event. God's action may seem overwhelming, yet he does not violate his free creature. The necessary condition whereby God's decrees are infallibly executed, yet the freedom of the creature is not thereby infringed, is Mary's "Immaculate Conception"—the fact that her freedom is free from any, from even the least, resistance against the decision of God's love; in other words, her creaturely freedom is exercised from and within uncreated, absolute freedom.

The "Immaculate Conception" is undoubtedly a personal privilege, but it is so as a function of the catholicity of her *fiat*, so that she can give her boundless assent—a priori and without knowing where it will lead her—to every hidden counsel of the saving will of God and so that afterward, from the same strength of her *fiat*, she can follow without resistance to the end of Jesus' path. Hence the need for her to be free from every, even the slightest, consequence of sin. Already, and from the start, she is expropriated—both in her own existence and then in the Yes within which this existence is articulated—into the saving work of God, so becoming within it a "generalized", "catholic" person. From the totality of the faith of Abraham and into the totality of the Christ event, she speaks her *fiat*, which, with womanly and creaturely limitations, assumes the same dimensions in her openness to whatever may happen as the manly and divine action of her Son. The Baptist seeks to set a boundary with the baptism of Jesus: "I need to be baptized by you!" Jesus must expressly remove this barrier: "Let it be so now" (Mt 3:14–15). Peter still more decidedly sets a boundary: "God forbid, Lord! This shall never happen to you", and Jesus must tear it down still more ruthlessly: "Get behind me, Satan! You are a hindrance to me" (Mt 16:22–23). Mary never sets a boundary; for as Mother she was too closely bound up with the fate of her Child to do so—in two ways. For as Mother she had the duty of raising her Child not only physically but also spiritually, while the Child, who was God's Son, had the duty of introducing the Mother into his divine-human fate.

The first of these aspects we see better today than did past generations, who sought, unhistorically and from the outset, to ascribe every divine and human perfection to the Child Jesus: omniscience, omnipotence. . . . They did not see that it is part of being a genuine human child to experience dependency upon his parents—that wonderful receptivity to being introduced by human beings to the tradition of being human. And since this Child owed his entire humanity to his Mother, it was likewise above all her task to initiate him into the religion of his fathers, into the attitude of Abraham's faith, into the understanding of the Commandments of God and of his promises through the prophets—while leaving it to God to show the Child just how much all these traditional and historical events were directed toward their fulfillment in him, the Child. Thus it was in Mary the Old Covenant that the New Covenant was introduced to its mission—albeit an Old Covenant that in its total openness had already crossed the threshold of the New and already possessed a dawning understanding of it. For just as in Abraham "all the nations" were to be blessed, so Mary knew that "all generations" would call her "blessed".

But the second aspect, the education of the Mother by the Child, ought to be by far the weightier and more difficult one. For who could have suspected, even after the songs of the Suffering Servant (which nobody dared to interpret) where the path of the Messiah was to lead? Since we do better to assume that Jesus himself had no precise foreknowledge of his path, even though he was willing to embrace his Father's will to the very utmost—or rather to see him as willing, for the sake of the higher good of obedience, to "deposit" all this foreknowledge with the Father—we should assume this to be still more the case with Mary. She, too, is ready for anything—somehow the fate of the Messiah had to be something unheard of—but what this "anything" will actually be, she does not know. And this very fact allows her entire life to go on beneath a cloud of anxiety. Even before the Son can personally instruct her, she is already being rehearsed: the shame of her pregnancy, the secret of which she is not permitted to reveal, the embarrassment of Joseph, gives her a bitter foretaste. The rejections in Bethlehem, when she had to give birth, and the subsequent flight likewise speak a symbolic language. This has already been made clear in the prophecy of the sword that will pierce her heart. And now it is the Son himself who wields this sword. As a twelve-year-old, he leaves her abruptly and, when she eventually finds him, gives her an answer that she does not understand. This incomprehension continues to loom menacingly over her life from now on. When the

Son does leave her, he certainly gives her no infor-
mation about what he is going to do, still less does
he send her any messages; she has to rely on rumors,
and more often than not distorted ones. In Cana,
there is the blunt rejection, when she is, after all,
concerned, in his spirit, for the poverty of their
hosts: his hour has not yet come; it does not coincide
with hers (only on the Cross will this be the case).
When his relatives think him crazy and she visits him
together with them, she is not received. She must
now function as a symbol of that "flesh and blood"
from which Jesus cuts himself off in order to establish a new relationship in the *pneuma* (her *fiat* is plas-
tic and elastic enough to accommodate itself even
to such a demonstration). And so it continues.
When the woman in the crowd praises the breasts
that suckled him, her words are immediately turned
around: "Blessed rather are those who hear the word
of God and keep it!" She, Mary, was the first to do
this, but now she disappears behind all those who
will have to imitate her in this; her human breasts,
which have nurtured the Word Incarnate, are now
not worthy of mention. Only for the final scene will
she be brought forth from obscurity and abandonment: she must be there beside the Cross, but not
in order to hear a final word of comfort; instead:
"Woman, behold your son!" Her Son, who has

moved farther and farther from her, now with-
draws from her entirely and foists another son on
her instead—she has no other form of communion
with him anymore except that which must now be:
just as he is abandoned by the Father, so his Mother
is abandoned by him—in this they are now one.

The Cross is the coinciding of their hours: the
hour of the Woman, who had always, and right from
her first *fiat*, given back the Son to the Father; and
of the Man, who at the end of his earthly mission
gives her and her spirit back to the Father. And until
this hour the Man had to educate the Woman, so
that everything could be brought to light that was
actually contained in her *fiat* and in the restitution
of it to God. What from the beginning was universal and catholic, because it was unlimited, must be
unfolded and imparted, in its explicit catholicity,
through the bitter, inexorable education imparted
by the Son. So now, at the Cross, the Mother is
mature enough to be more than merely the Mother
of this one Son; now she can become the Mother
of other sons, of all those who through the advo-
cacy of Jesus have become his brothers and co-heirs
(Rom 8:17; 29). That she must become so is a consequence implicit in her first motherhood. One cannot "with impunity" be the Mother of the One
who must take the last place among men in order

to be able to bring in the very last sinner of all and free him from the solitude of his sin. For in saying Yes to this motherhood, she intended, not only something physical, but the whole of this Child—and not simply by virtue of a touchingly human motherly love, but because this Yes to the Child was identical to Abraham's act of faith, identical with the assent to every one of the salvific paths upon which God wills and must take man along, too, so that he can be saved, not simply externally, but from within, in his freedom. Thus Mary cannot be Mother of the Messiah without becoming Mother of all the brothers of the Messiah (Rev 12:17), without therefore being the co-origin of the Church, of which it is said that she flows out from the opened side of the Crucified.

Here the mystery becomes very dense. For this Church, which proceeds from the side of the New Adam, just as Eve did from the side of the sleeping first Adam, was yet already at least inchoately present in the universal *fiat* of the Mother. This perfect accompanying of the "man" by the companion is precisely what God the Creator desired to give to the first Adam and God the Redeemer to the second. Hence we must say both things: that beneath the Cross Mary becomes the Church ("behold, your son") and that, as the Mother of Christ, she has already made her contribution to the formation of this Church. For if the first Eve is entirely from the man, then the second Adam is from the Woman (1 Cor 11:12), yet "all things are from God." Here the cycle that links man and woman, child and mother has become indissoluble, and this cycle makes necessary the concept of the "anticipated redemption" of the Mother, which makes it possible for Mary, although redeemed by the Cross, to be at the same time, as a servant, a contributory cause of the redeemer. In no sense is the difference between God and creature thereby encroached upon. Instead, it becomes evident just why Mary, too, had to be educated by the Son for the "last place". For it is only in this place, where the last of all sinners are gathered in, that the redemption takes place, and only in this place that the Church, which must bear the mind of Christ throughout history, can embrace her role, understand it, and persevere in it.

It is a place that the Son can assume only in death (between the two thieves) and one in which the Mother can be established only as the virginal one (meaning, in Old Testament terms, the shamefully unfruitful one). For as the Mother she must now also simultaneously assume the role of the "companion", of the Bride, and of the Church—newly fruitful with the virginal, eucharistic fertility of Christ's Cross—something that is possible only if no human father has ever stood here, whose place (as in the Oedipus myth) might subsequently be taken by the son. On the Cross the *absolute* relationship—transcending the sexual—between man and woman is brought to light, whereby the man can and must be at once child and bridegroom, the woman at once mother and bride. This is something that is absolutely possible only beyond the sexual level, at the level of virginity and its supernatural fruitfulness. From this perspective, the Woman of the Apocalypse can be interpreted as representing the Old Testament People of God, from whom the Messiah will issue—provided we discern the living pinnacle of this people, this inchoate Church, in Mary, who gives birth to him from whom "Church" in her fullest sense arises in the first place—with retrospective effect of course, right back to the origins of the *Civitas Dei*, as clearly revealed in the status of the Lamb in the Apocalypse, who governs all world history, of Old and New Testament alike.

But there is something else that is illuminated by Mary's position at the foot of the Cross, something that has a bearing on what follows, on what is said about Peter. We speak of the Sacrifice of the Cross, and rightly so—in a fulfilling and exalted sense—insofar as Jesus dedicates himself as the Victim offered in the name of all sinners (Jn 17:19) in order, in this way and in accordance with the will of the Father, to establish peace in heaven and on earth and so enable his desire for reconciliation to take effect (Col 1:20; 2 Cor 5:19). His is a sacrifice that in the burning fire of suffering consumes within itself the entire godforsakenness of the sinner—and thus it is not only the most physically but also the most spiritually agonizing sacrifice of all. What, then, is Mary's position now in relation to this divine and human sacrifice (inasmuch as she is also the origin and heart of the Church)? She embraces it with him, since she does not revoke her Yes (*fiat*) but remains faithful to it to the last. She lets it be done. She offers to the Father, as she has always done, this self-sacrificing, sacrificial Victim, but in such a way that this offering (*oblatio*) is for her the most heartrending renunciation, only thereby making her oblation truly into a sacrifice, the surrender of what is dearest of all. How much sooner would the Mother suffer in the place of her Son all that he has to undergo! How terrible it is to have to assent to this sacrifice, which, from a worldly perspective, is the most meaningless and hopeless of all! And when in Holy Mass, during the Canon, the Church again and again speaks of a sacrifice offered and recalls that it is not only the sacrifice of the Son that is commemorated but that the Church herself fully participates in the act of sacrifice, where else has she truly realized what this, her offering to the Father of the Son, costs *her* except at that moment when, in Mary, she offered up her Son to the Father? Sinners in the Church cannot in fact realize this; they must be glad, rather, that Christ offers himself for them. And Church does not exist except in real subjects. Alone, this all-holy woman, and at most just a few others who have been purified to the point of purest love, can gauge what sword it is that pierces the heart of the Church when she for her part *sacrifices* to the Father this self-sacrificing Lamb.

2. Peter-Church

In the public life of the Lord, the foundations were laid for the Church that was ultimately to be founded through his death and his Resurrection. A Church that—as we have seen—had already begun to exist in Nazareth, in secret and in a manner inaccessible to the disciples, but which now had to assume a visible and public form. For just as for the Incarnation of the Word, the *fiat* of a woman was necessary—an ecclesial community in embryo—so it corresponds

to the human form of the Word that it be made
present in an objective and social, "institutional",
form and remain thus accessible through the ages.
Christ is there not only for each separate individual in purely inward, private matters; he is present
also in the public sphere, in what he offers and what
he demands, and must therefore also have a public
form. The written account of him is not just some
unclaimed work making the rounds of secondhand
bookstores. The Bible is the book of the Church,
a book that *she* understands, proclaims, and inter-
prets; a book that in its totality can only be misun-
derstood outside of her, since in speaking of God
and of Christ it at the same time speaks of the
Church herself.

Yet this visible institution is not some abstract
thing but is, rather, something, once again, made
concrete in and through men in real and sacramental symbolism—by the Twelve, with Peter in their
midst as the rock upon whom the edifice is built.
And let us be clear: the promise made to Peter
(which Matthew places at the moment of Peter's
first confession of the Messiah but which may pos-
sibly have been spoken only after the Easter event)
already presupposes the call of the Twelve, their
willingness to leave everything and follow him. The
words of institution and priestly authority only

come later, in second place, preceded by the actual, existential sharing in the life of Jesus. A somewhat naive and as yet unreflecting faith that only later—in the question "Who do you say that I am?" and in the response of Peter, as representative of them all— matures into a clarified and considered faith. If we leave the text where Matthew places it, then this reflection is still only in its infancy, and the abrupt shift from Peter's confession about the Messiah to the promise, which immediately follows, of the Passion and death of the Son of Man—which Peter rejects—shows just how far this faith still has to go.

Nevertheless, this faith can already be designated in advance as the rock upon which the house of Christ will be built. It is not shifting sand, for otherwise the house would collapse under the assault of hell (Mt 7:26f.). It has the quality of the rock that in John's Gospel was already attributed to Peter by the Lord on their first encounter—a quality given from above into the human sand of this man; a quality one can define as "infallibility", or "that which cannot fail" in what is essential. Thus Peter, as the established rock, will also be the one who, after the great collapse of the Passion, will have to strengthen his brothers in their faith (Lk 22:32). In him the act of foundation, or commission, has a power that is mightier than the person: "You are

Simon, but you *will* be Peter": again, the sovereign
future tense. He is the prisoner of his mission,
which seems and also is too great for him: "Depart
from me, for I am a sinful man, O Lord"—and
which has seized him, along with his sense of
unworthiness: "Do not fear, from now on you *will*
be catching men" (Lk 5:8–10). But what Peter must
know about himself is also in the same future tense:
"You *will* deny me three times." Without this humbling of his sinful presumption, he cannot advance
to the unconditional embracing of his mission.
Again, at the washing of the feet, he thinks he
knows better—the idea that the Master should
humble himself before his disciples undermines the
world order. He does not understand, but then right
now he does not need to understand: "What I am
doing you do not know now, but afterward you *will*
understand" (Jn 13:7). Just as he must seek to build,
not at all on the basis of his own abilities, but,
rather, on the basis of the ever-present disposition
of the Lord: "Where I am going you cannot follow me now; but you *shall* follow afterward" (Jn
13:36). In the hour of decision of Christ's suffering, the failure of Peter must become public—the
Passion of Jesus is the forced confession of his
Church: the interfering with the this-worldly sword,
when humble acceptance was called for; the

thrice-repeated denial and, in consequence of it, the bitter weeping in a corner, far from the decisive events of the Cross. Yet the humiliation of the failure to be present becomes the precondition for the final promise—that he will follow "later", to the place where "you do not wish to go"; to a cross that is both communion with and separation from the Lord, since the servant will be crucified upside down, a sort of mirror image. The final humiliation is the most profound—for in order to be able to follow the Chief Shepherd in the pasturing of his flock, he must respond three times to the question "Do you love me *more* than these?" In light of his recent denials, this "more" is an unbearable thorn for the personal humanity of Simon, one that he can answer only from the perspective of his mission, which expropriates him and situates him in the Church, as *Communio Sanctorum*, and thus enables him, from within this communion (the beloved disciple standing beside him), to respond with Yes. As the one sent, he is dependent on the holy, the loving, the Marian Church.

The Eucharist of the Lord, the fruit of his Passion, is entrusted to Peter and to the other disciples. Yet essentially this celebration over which he presides remains for him an ever-new reminder of his failure—for he now offers to the Father, in the name of the Church, what he failed to offer during his hour of decision. He must offer it—if the Church's offering is truly to be a communion with the self-offering of Christ—in the spirit of Mary. The sinful, the denying, the bitterly weeping Church could not offer up the self-offering Son to the Father unless she knew herself to be sustained by the immaculate Church. And when, still in the presence of the community, Peter and the other members of the ministerial priesthood receive back from the Father the Victim now transformed into the Body and Blood of Christ, then again they can fittingly receive the gift only if, behind the unworthy and inadequate servants (*Domine, non sum dignus*), there stands the *Ecclesia immaculata*, who alone has known how to welcome within herself the incarnating Word of God in all his fullness.

Here we see (by means of a central example, though this truth is everywhere present) the extent to which the action of Mary is no unique, past historical event, but, rather, is present throughout the whole history of the Church and, indeed, mediated by the action of her Son in making himself perpetually present. Because he continues constantly to offer himself anew, he likewise continues constantly to be offered up by the Mother. Because he allows himself to be received again and again anew by believing but imperfect souls, the perfect reception in Mary remains forever current. And as we have seen, this reception of hers was so perfect because it was done in self-expropriation for the sake of all and in the name of all and, thus, within the unique event was already included the ever-recurring one.

3. The Mediation

What was just said already shows that there are not two churches—an inner, holy, hidden one and an external, sinful, visible one. Mary and Peter are two "real symbols" of the one and only Church. But are not both figures entirely separate in the Gospels? There is one figure that unites them, and this unification is effected by Jesus himself.

Beneath the Cross, Mary stands with the disciple whom Jesus loves. To this disciple Jesus hands over his Mother. And not only figuratively, but literally—he is to take her into his house; he is to shelter the *Ecclesia immaculata* in his own home. As a son, he is to acknowledge her motherhood over him and those like him. But this disciple is also the companion of Peter. In the Cenacle he mediates between Peter and the Lord. With Peter he hastens to the tomb and makes way for him—as the figure of authority—to enter first. When fishing on the lake, he recognizes the Lord and communicates what he sees to Peter. He recounts, in a crowning moment of his Gospel, the ultimate investiture of Peter and the promise of his crucifixion. At the beginning of the Acts of the Apostles, he appears constantly by Peter's side, inseparable from him. Along with Peter and James, he is regarded by Paul as a pillar of the Church. And at the end of his Apocalypse, he will see the two sides of the Church in perfect unity: the spotless Bride of the Lamb, shown to him by the angel, is at the same time the Holy City, with the twelve foundation stones upon which are inscribed the names of the twelve apostles of the Lamb (Acts 21:9, 14). John is the theologian of the Church, insofar as she is Marian and insofar as she is Petrine.

At the same time it should not be forgotten that John is no isolated bridge, for beneath the Cross there also stands Magdalen, a "real symbol" of the once sinful Church, now washed by the Blood of Christ (Eph 5:26), the *casta meretrix*, as Ambrose calls the Church. There, too, are the other holy women, mothers and representatives of their apostolic sons, just as prayerful and loving women always stand behind ordained priests. Thus the great "real symbols" are already embedded within ecclesial community.

Now we can cast a concluding glance at the very mysterious relationship of the sexes within the

Church. The priest, as a man, stands initially in the region of Peter; he participates in his mission of representing the Lord with regard to the "feminine" Church and community. Yet Peter's role in the Gospel becomes effective only long after that of Mary; the origin of the Church lies, not in the calling of the apostles, but in the private room in Nazareth, when the Yes of the Son to the Father became communion with the Yes of the Mother to the Incarnation. And again, the origin of the Church lies beneath the Cross, where the female *Ecclesia*—as she is depicted in the Middle Ages—fills her chalice from the wound in the side of Christ in order then to pass it on to the male officials. When Mary gives her Son to the Church, she gives her something of the priestly office that, however, resides, *not in her*, Mary, but in the Son. In no sense can a community give an individual, even to one it may itself have designated, the power of office that is always bestowed by the Lord, through Peter and his successors and brothers in office. Nonetheless, the ministerial (male) Church does not stand in direct contrast to the loving (female) Church. For after all, Peter—in John's portrayal (and through John's renunciation of a privileged friendship with the Lord)—is exhorted by virtue of his office to "greater love", since only so can he become the successor to the Good Shepherd. For Jesus is

Shepherd and Priest only because he lays down his life for his sheep—in other words, in a unique manner that unifies the one who offers the sacrifice (the Priest) with the sacrificial victim (the Lamb). It is one of the greatest paradoxes of revelation that this entirely singular and unique office—so different from the priesthood of Aaron and the shepherd's role of the Old Testament kings—is actually passed on by Jesus. He alone can ensure that even in the most extreme case—at the moment of death, even in Peter, even in the priest—ministry and love can coincide. Thus every successor of Peter, every priest, must live in the perspective of this borderline identity.

On the other hand, the validity of the ecclesial office cannot be measured against this borderline case—that would be Donatism. According to the will of Jesus, the validity of the priestly ministry lies in its ultimate independence of the worthiness of the minister, and to this extent it must be covered in its deficiency from elsewhere—needless to say, first of all by the eternal and perfect High Priest, Christ, but at the same time also by the *Ecclesia immaculata mariana*. By both of them.

Yet we must still cast a more realistic glance at the relationship between the sexes. From the perspective of natural sexuality, the role that falls to the man is of vanishingly small significance: that of initiating the great process of fruitfulness in the woman. She is of course the recipient of the seed, but in an active reception that shows the full range of its activity in pregnancy, birth, and nurturing of the child. Yet ultimately, the gender relationship within the Church is to be interpreted, not from the perspective of natural sexuality, but from that of the supernatural and virginal relationship between Christ and the Church—this is the great mystery between man and woman, the *Analogatum princeps* from which (according to Ephesians 5) the natural male-female relationship derives its dignity. And at this higher level, the fruitfulness of the woman is the consequence of the unique divine-human fruitfulness of Jesus Christ, who—as the perfect image of the eternal fruitfulness of the divine Father in the world—can pour out his entire body as a generative principle into the Church. Or who, more precisely, through the Eucharistic self-outpouring of his own fullness, first of all generates the vessel, the Church, as the representation of his own fullness (Eph 1:23). Accordingly, Mary (as a "real symbol" of the Church) is redeemed, in anticipation, from the Cross—just as Eve was "flesh of my flesh" to Adam, in order to become his helpmate. To this extent the entire fruitfulness of the body of the Church—both Marian and Petrine—springs from the Head, Christ, even if it remains true that the ministry of the Church is still dependent on the intercession of the holy Church[1]—just as the holy Church remains ordered to the objectively mediating ministry.

Only here there is a final misunderstanding to be avoided. The ministry, which in a certain sense is the "objective spirit" of holiness, is therefore never to be detached from the subjective Marian spirit of holiness. The objectivity of the ministry is derived in the Church from the subjectivity of Christ's achievement on the Cross and remains always covered by it. The male priesthood is, as it were, crystallized divine love—for the sake of the female community, which, through this form of love, is able to come into direct contact with the Lord and with the triune God.

In the Son himself, however, the subjective love for the Father was so perfect that it was able to

[1] In this regard, the theory of Cardinal Mercier is altogether unacceptable, which sees the diocesan clergy as the real "state of perfection" established by Christ, whereas the various religious orders, which also include women, are only secondarily derived. Women rightly protest against such a one-sided view, and—if the theory were true—they would not be unjustified in aiming at participation in the ministerial priesthood. All our explanations show, however, just how inappropriate such an aim is. But there is a real need for an expressly Marian view of the Church, so that all arrogance within her—whether of male officials or of allegedly discriminated against women—can be judged by the humility of the lowly Handmaid. *Deposuit potentes de sede.*

empty itself out completely into the pure objectivity of his obedience unto death. The final unity of both aspects of love reveals to us the mystery of the Person of the Holy Spirit. For the Holy Spirit makes possible this unity in duality, since in the work of redemption he is both things at once—the everlasting subjective love between the Father and the Son-made-man and the objective witness to this love at the very heart of the Trinity. It is he who then presents to the incarnate Son the will of the Father as an objective rule—even to the extent of its iron necessity in regard to the Passion. The Spirit is love as ministry and ministry as love.

Thus the unity of the Church is rooted, like the unity between Mary and Peter—between Jerusalem as the Bride and the geometrically constructed city built on the foundation stones of the apostles—entirely in the mystery of the economic and, ultimately, the immanent Trinity.

THE PRIEST I SEEK

I

If we are sick, we go to the doctor; if making a will, we go to a lawyer—in short, to an expert. But is there an expert for God's relationship with me? God is subject to no laws in his free gift to a person. Neither the sociologist nor the psychologist has lost anything here; their object is at best the average religious behavior of the "human species" toward a so-called Absolute. But then I, too—this unique individual to whom the unique God turns—am subject to no general law. Thus, in my relationship to God, which must be guided by God's relationship to me, I am alone; no one else has insight, can explain or mediate. Just as each of us dies alone, so too he ultimately prays alone, must enter his "chamber" before his Father in heaven, must seek to understand and follow God's will for him and him alone. "There is no one else to stand up for him."

God's Word has become flesh and comes to meet each man, the blind, the lame, the deaf, in Jesus Christ.

63

Always as the unique Word. The command to follow him is directed to the tax collector Levi, not to the others sitting beside him. There is no socio-psychological law governing the behavior of Jesus or of those whom he addresses when they are exposed to his free, unique claim. If those thus addressed consider the normal laws of human behavior—saying farewell, burying one's father, and so on—then this seems wrong; for then they are "not worthy of him". I cannot simply set off God's word to me against the famous "concrete situation" so that a sort of parallelogram of forces results from the two.

Jesus, the Word of God for me, comes to meet me in the Church, which preserves his Word as ever alive today in proclamation and sacrament—and both of these belong together, for example when the words *ego te absolvo a peccatis tuis* are spoken to me. It encounters me in the Church, within whose communion I am to receive the assurance that God's Word will ring out to me, not from the far-distant past, but as close and engaging and unequivocal as my presence here and now is concrete. But does not the Church then become once more a general law that in its interpretation of the unique will of God for me places itself between God and me, informed by her perhaps unique, centuries-old socio-psychological experience? "In such and such a case, God usually means this and that." In that case, then I and, ultimately, God himself would have been reduced to an anonymous factor, and I, in order to discover my own personal fate, would have to leave such a church.

And yet, if Church as *Ekklesia* is the community of those called, if the Word of God and the keys to the Kingdom of heaven have been entrusted to her, if the gift of the Holy Spirit has been given her by God and by Jesus Christ—the Spirit who as God is just as unique as the Father and the Son and can interpret for us premordially the will of the Father in the Son—how am I not to be referred to the Church if I seek to plan my life under the truth of the living God? But which Church? Who in the Church can help me? I, too, am a member of the Church, but I can neither claim for myself the Holy Spirit in his ecclesial fullness nor sincerely describe myself as a "good Christian" who lives close to the heart of the Church and communicates by osmosis with her most inward understanding. Instead, if I am honest, I know very precisely just how far I fall short of the demands of God and how gladly I would like to reduce these demands to the level of my average, middle-class, sinful, and broken down level and, against my better judgment, to give the last word to religious sociology: "That's the way men are", or "On the whole, and given my personal dispositions, they can't ask any more of me."

2

How difficult and muddled the situation of the person looking for help seems from the foregoing. Can the demands I am making actually be satisfied by any man? He would have to mediate on my behalf in my unique relationship with God, without, however, dissolving this relationship in inner-worldly generalities. He would therefore have to know, from his own unique relationship with God, what this uniqueness actually is and at the same time be equipped with the mission and the authority to be able to know this, in the Holy Spirit, for others, also, and to give them the appropriate guidance. Mission and authority from God, combined with experience in the Spirit: this would give him the capacity to demand of me—not for himself, but for God and for me—what I do not trust myself to demand of myself.

This is the first quality he would have to have, the priest I seek—for he would have to be a priest, or at any rate someone commissioned and authorized from above, by Christ, to hold out to me

God's Incarnate Word, so that I can be sure that I cannot dispose of it myself, that I have not already emasculated it in advance by psychologizing, interpreting, de-mythologizing it in such a way that it can no longer generate in me what it wishes; in such a way that I cannot escape its demands because they come to me in the concrete form of ecclesial authority, which through its ministry actualizes the concrete reality of the divine. But it is not enough for someone to confront me inexorably with the demands of the Word, only then to leave me standing there. Maybe I have already got as far as this demand by myself. He must also help me to persevere and not to run away by staying alongside me with an unwavering love. With a terrifying love that says to me again and again: "This is after all what you actually want." A love that deserves our most profound gratitude, for it is simply irreplaceable. At certain moments, such a person is like the angel on the Mount of Olives, strengthening us to be alone with God. The strength with which such a person does this stems partly of course from his mission (which has within it the strength and relentlessness of God); but it also springs from his own strength that has grown within him through his being alone with God. Simultaneously, from his mission and from experience, he can embody both aspects—the inexorability and the love that lies within the will of God—so that we no longer wish or are able to run away.

Were he lacking in experience, then he could not even credibly proclaim the Word of God from the pulpit; he could at best be a lifeless echo of what others (like Paul, for example) have proclaimed of the Word of God in their existence. Still less would he be capable of existentially accompanying the believer in the existential confrontation with the Word of God and of holding him within it. "Were he lacking in experience . . ."—the word "specialist" springs to mind at this point and must be immediately rejected. For in the one who is ever unique there can be no special "fields", no classifications. Even words like "science" must be avoided. At most one can speak of a certain "wisdom" that the Holy Spirit imparts to those who are familiar with his "blowing where he wills". Of course there are "rules for the discernment of spirits" that have been established, and people have spoken of a "science of the saints", but such rules, if they are genuine and useful, are always transmitted from personal experience within the Church into personal experience, and this "science" is to be understood as one of the Seven Gifts of the Holy Spirit and thus only translatable and comprehensible to those who strive, in prayer and the living of their lives, to enter into the medium of the Spirit.

3

And so, for the man who assumes the task within the Church of officially proclaiming the Word of God that is Christ and presenting it to each and every individual, there can be no other way of doing so consistently and of persevering in this task than by totally committing his existence to this mission. He must identify himself with it. This is what the apostles did, at Jesus' behest, when they left everything to follow him—not just house and home, but wife and children, too. Of course, this material letting go in order to commit their lives to the Word of God is still only the starting point; it does not become the criterion for "the priest I seek" until this first step becomes a sustained way of life. From a worldly perspective, such a way of life is and remains meaningless since it cannot be reinterpreted in terms of a sociological state of life; and where an attempt was made to justify such an ecclesial status on the basis of paganism or Judaism, it remained a questionable one. The priest must always expect to be excluded again from the organization of society. Here, if anywhere, Saint

Augustine's words hold good, to the effect that whoever bases his life on Christ does not stand but hangs or "stands above himself". And only through God in Christ can we have the assurance that whoever leaves everything "for my sake and the gospel's" does not fall into the void, does not fall between two stools, but is carried (hanging) all the way through his impossible existence. Clearly, such a person cannot have any "self-understanding", since he has given up interpreting himself in order to be interpreted by God alone. He does not "judge himself" but holds himself oriented toward God, who recognizes him and judges him. As a man who has renounced his self-understanding, he is the priest I seek and who, by his existence, can become for me a word and light of God. This abandonment of existence, along with its own lights—and only this—can guarantee the essential humility that allows him to be permeated by a light other than his own and to radiate something that neither interests the one thus dedicated nor is something on which he reflects or that he cultivates. The fire that burns in the humble man is the fire of love for God and his incarnate Word; its source lies not in him but in that which he loves, and it is kindled by the thought that Love, God, is not loved in this world, that men despise it or are scandalized by its weakness. "Who is made to fall, and I am not indignant?" Humility and zeal grow together.

The humble priest will not be tempted to hold up to me as an example anything other than God's Word for me. The zealous priest will not permit me to run away because of this Word. He makes me stick to it, and I can accuse him of being too demanding, in reality it is only the Word of God itself that is demanding and forceful. When I find the one I seek, I cannot reproach him for behaving toward me with a confident assurance that does not befit a man. As though he is permitted only to express suggestions about the direction in which my path to God might perhaps be tend, but must leave it to me and my personal conscience to test these suggestions and either accept or reject them. His mission allows him no false modesty, assuming he has surrendered his existence for the sake of his priestly authority. If not, he will not exercise authority in the Church except in a partial and tarnished way. But if the transparency, the devotion, of his prayer in union with God, of his humility in transmitting it, is truly achieved, then too the miracle can happen whereby, within the ecclesial Holy Spirit, genuine instruction from God is imparted, which I—however uncomfortable it may be—cannot ignore. To the simple and self-effacing alone is entrusted the grace of certainty. He can be joyous with the joyful, can weep with those who weep, but he is never permitted to falter in solidarity with the faltering and uncertain. His experience with God has taught him what that darkness is in which one can only grope one's way along the walls, and even these walls will occasionally recede in the darkness, leaving one to flounder in the empty void. Such experience is granted to the priest so that he can endure, humbly, but as a source of strength for his brother.

4

We spoke just now of a miracle. That a priest should succeed is always a miracle of grace. More often it happens that the Churches have to suffer the results of failure. There are too many who speak from lectern or pulpit imagining themselves to be of the light. They are to be avoided. They speak of God but mean themselves; God does not actually make an appearance. Whether they declare him dead or alive or claim to know too much or too little about him is almost irrelevant. There are others who dream up ways of attracting people's attention to themselves; they have language problems; they think that if people suddenly hear them speaking of God in their own worldly language, they will listen again and understand something—a manipulated Pentecost miracle, as it were. By their own ranks they are admired, but by those they seek to win over they are despised. They have nothing to tell them. And then there are the defectors, who were called to a life conformed to Jesus Christ but were afraid they could no longer get through to men and short-circuited, allowing the love of God to be lost in the love of neighbor. And so they have nothing more to proclaim and no authority to demand of men anything more than is already contained within their self-understanding. They dissolve into the anonymity of the human. And finally there are the anxious ones who, the more the inherited forms are dropped, the more tightly they cling to those that are left. To be sure, they know that the Spirit incarnates himself in historical forms, but they lack the freedom to allow him to blow where he wills and confuse him with the forms themselves. With their antitheses, they lend credence to the theses that are overtaking them.

The miracle we are looking out for would perhaps be nothing other than holiness—the holiness of the man who in God has become so insignificant to himself that for him only God now matters. Who he himself is no longer concerns him. That is why he is as ordinary and nourishing as a loaf of bread, from which anyone can break off a piece for himself. The manner in which he distributes himself merges into the way in which God's Word is distributed in bread and wine. Such a man also knows how to break open God's Word and interpret it. He will not send me home from the desert, like the preachers of today, with an indigestible supply of empty phrases about the openness of the Church to the world. What am I to serve the hungry around me if not bread? Yet where am I to get it if it is not first given to me? How is the Church to go out to the world if she has nothing left within to dispose of? Or does she project from within herself the uncertainty about her own identity because she no longer has any experience of what her true inner reality is? For this inner reality is not she herself—Church cannot reflect herself—but Christ, her Head and her Soul, through whom the triune God dwells within her.

In earlier times there were the monks. In East and West, on Mount Athos, in Clairvaux and in Ranft, in Kiev and Optina. They experienced, and they knew. They gave instruction. Their light was bread. They came from deep within as far as the threshold, where their experience crystallized into a given word. Perhaps such external seclusion is not absolutely essential in order to know what is within; there is solitude enough blowing through the spaces between men. Yet their emptiness is not automatically filled with precious content. Even in the hopeless emptiness of another human heart, I find the sacred mystery of divine poverty only if I have already sought it, already bring it with me, if it has already been opened up to me. Otherwise, one empty void merely encounters another, and the Word does not sustain but collapses, lifeless and helpless.

Priests are commonly called [in German] *die Geistlichen* [spiritual ones] or, in Greek, *Pneumatikoi*—a word also used to describe monks. In the Orthodox faith, for centuries it has always been the monastic orders that have supplied the candidates for the higher ranks of the hierarchy. Spiritual men are those who have experience in the Holy Spirit and who, from this experience, are able to recognize the hidden, unrecognized, and unliberated spirit in us, in me, and enkindle it. How rare these spiritual men have become! Must we therefore make do with an *ersatz* spirituality? Such a substitute spirituality is offered above all by psychology—though this is not to say that a good, humble psychologist cannot be open to the Holy Spirit—but its subject is, after all, the general laws of the human psyche. The Spirit by contrast is always unique. The spiritual man must allow the unique Spirit to work through him, so that he can meet the need of this unique individual who stands before him. Not through the exercise of mediumistic powers, but opened to the grace of the living God, who in freedom speaks to me his Word of Love, kindly and firm—through the priest whom I seek.

We are not forgetting the sacramental grace of the priestly ministry. It helps in the process of self-emptying. But it does not replace it. If the ordained minister does not open himself up to that grace, he is negatively marked by it. There is a particular kind of un-spirituality that only the wayward "spiritual one" can display—stupid, sly, busy, and importunate. He wants to be heard, he pushes himself into the media. He lies like mildew on the fields of today's Church. Perhaps only necessity will teach these "spiritual ones" to pray once again. Meanwhile, let us pray for them.

OFFICE AND EXISTENCE

Whoever holds an office has the power to exercise authority, to give commands on behalf of the community. In a democracy the exercise of an office is subject to the control of those who obey it. They have elected the official and conferred authority on him; therefore they determine to what extent the exercise of this office corresponds to the service of the common good. Their obedience is thus a critical obedience; it does not in principle go beyond the insight of those who obey. This model does not apply to the constitution of the Old and New Testament People of God, which is not democratic but theocratic and Christocratic. For here the authority is bestowed, not by the people, but by God and by Christ. This holds good for the entire biblical realm, to the scope of which we are limiting ourselves in this study, but with the intention of thereby throwing light on two contemporary questions: Is there a Christian exercise of authority that is not backed up by the life of the officeholder? Do those who obey have a critical function even if the conferral of authority does not emanate from them?

1. In the Broad Context of the Bible

All the principal figures who carry forward the action of the Old and New Testaments are characterized by unity of mission and life. Their mission always proceeds from God. And the whole being of the person to whom it has been entrusted is always demanded in this mission. The act by which he makes himself available for it—whether we call it faith, trust, obedience, letting oneself be guided, or whatever—dispossesses him, right down to his most private sphere, for the sake of his service, which is always a service to the People of God. Expropriated from himself and in his office, the one commissioned assumes an existential responsibility in unlimited obedience. We see in Moses that the slightest disobedience or lack of faith in regard to God is severely punished, because the grave responsibility for the distressed and quarrelsome people cannot for one moment be allowed to depend on private considerations but must always remain the expression of God's will. This can only happen if the one commissioned remains in living contact, through prayerful obedience, with the God who commissions him.

Such is the kind of contact that Abraham has with God, upon whose promise his entire existence is based, in faith, for the sake of his future descendants— even to the point of blind obedience that is ready to sacrifice the son of the promise without "critically" accusing God of contradiction. Moses' stubborn will-fulness is broken by God in the account of his call-ing; otherwise, he could have become neither the mediator between God and the people nor the wise leader of the people. Joshua is designated by Yah-weh as the rightful successor, "in whom is the spirit", upon whom Moses is to lay his hand (Num 27:18), and Yahweh instructs Joshua himself to "meditate . . . day and night" on the book of the Law, "that you may be careful to do according to all that is written in it" (Josh 1:8). Likewise it is Yahweh who "raised up judges" and "was with the judge" and who sud-denly came upon him with his Spirit (cf. Judg 2:16, 18; 3:10, and so on). As the sociological structures of the people stabilize, it is he who chooses the king, who deposes him when his obedience is not perfect and replaces him with another and better king ("I have provided for myself a king", 1 Sam 16:1). And when God guarantees the dynasty beginning with David, he does not do so without the proviso that if any one of his offspring should separate office from obedience, he will chasten him "with the rod of men,

with the stripes of the sons of men" (2 Sam 7:14).
The institution of the priestly office is based on an
analogous total consecration of life (the decision for
Yahweh: Deut 33:8ff.; the offering up of the Lev-
ites instead of the firstborn, who belong to Yahweh: Num 3:12ff.; no share in the land: "the Lord
God of Israel is their inheritance" Jos 13:33).[1] And
if the origins of prophecy lie shrouded in darkness—
though nevertheless the life of the prophet appears
right from the start to be a way of life (cf. 1 Sam
19:20)—yet the prophetic mission is one that totally
consumes an Elijah, and in the case of the great
prophets of Scripture the demands of the word of
God bore ever deeper into the personal life of the
prophet concerned (Jeremiah, Ezekiel), until the
image of the ideal hearer of the word emerges
(Is 50:4) who not only truly performs the word but
also perfectly suffers it—foreshadowing the coming Redeemer.

This Redeemer, Jesus Christ, is purely and simply the identity of office and existence, the mission
personified: the Word of the Father as Son, and the
Son of the Father as his Word. That these two aspects
could at any time be imagined to be unlinked in him

---

[1] We are considering here, throughout, the history of Israel as it
was formulated from the perspective of its own theological self-
understanding. Only this normative picture is taken into consideration.

is ever more categorically excluded by the reflection of the New Testament authors upon his being and his history. He is and knows himself to be and announces himself as the Word made flesh. This is completed in the paradox that in his mediating Passion he is at once both Priest and Victim—the officially authorized executor and the existential sufferer of the ultimate (of abandonment by God). If, after him, there is once again to be official authority in his Church—and he himself has expressly conferred such authority (Mk 3:15; 6:7; Mt 10:1; Lk 9:19; Mt 16:19; Jn 21:15ff.)—then this can occur only in the closest connection with a form of existence that must, on the one hand, demand total availability for the mission (Mt 8:18ff., and so on), yet, on the other hand, be still more a promise. For the very highest representative of ecclesial office is the one to whom death on the Cross is promised (Jn 21:19). And in the high-priestly prayer of Christ, the apostles with him are "consecrated in the truth" in the same consecration of life and sacrifice as that of Jesus (Jn 17:17; 19). From the perspective of the official priest of the New Covenant, Jesus, such a participation in his priest-victim identity by the officeholders who will follow him is nothing optional, accidental, or inordinate, but is, rather, the mark (*stigma*) of New Testament office. Somehow, the later heretics, like the

Montanists and the Donatists, felt rightly—even though they drew the false conclusion from it—that a Christian priest who does not live the sanctity of his office in his actual existence is incapable of conveying the grace of Christ to the people of God. That he is theologically a "monster", an "impossible possibility", is clear to all. Yet this monster is not granted so much power that he can destroy the work of Christ or the existence of his Church. Finally, the life and writings of Saint Paul attest to the possibility, in the imitation Christ, of bringing the official authority into harmony with life, and Paul remains the model for every subsequent office. Timothy adopted him as his model and "observed my teaching, my conduct, my aim in life, my faith, my patience, my love, my steadfastness, my persecutions, my sufferings" (2 Tim 3:10–11). Paul constantly uses his own life as an argument, as a demonstration of the teaching he proclaims, even though he in no way seeks to equate himself with Christ; he is merely an "ambassador" for Christ (2 Cor 5:20), though still his "fellow worker" (he also says the same thing of the other officeholders, for example, Rom 16:21; 1 Cor 3:9; 16:16; 2 Cor 8:23; Phil 2:25; 4:3). From the grace of his election and in the devotion of his faith, he participates in the identity of office and existence that is present in and is communicated by Christ.

2. The Identity in Christ

So far we have seen the continuity from Abraham and Moses through to Paul: no important office is bestowed by God in the biblical context without its bearer having placed his entire existence at God's disposal. But this consistent underlying law undergoes an intensification as it passes from the Old to the New Covenant, caused by the fact that Israel was a "fleshly" people, whereas the Church is the "spiritual Israel". At that time, sociological legalities were still operative, but these disappear with Jesus. The Letter to the Hebrews starkly and almost one-sidedly[2] stresses the rupture: the institutional, Old Covenant priesthood has been abolished in the utterly unique and, hence, once-for-all, existential priesthood of Christ. But this necessary observation does not seek to deny either that there was already an interrelationship, even in the Old Covenant, between office and existence or that it will be possible in the New Covenant for such an existence to embody a particular official ministry. It seeks only to put an end

[2] With regard to the visible corrections present in the Letter to the Hebrews itself and in the rest of the New Testament, cf. Heribert Mühlen, *Entsakralisierung* (Schöningh, 1971), 283ff., and also the report of the International Theological Commission on *The Priestly Ministry*, trans. Jacques Dupuis (Bangalore: Theological Publications in India, 1971).

to the national, impersonal institution—such as the inherited priesthood and kingship. If, among the ancient peoples, the king was regarded as inspired solely by virtue of his office, and if the priest in Israel—solely on the basis of his inherited function—possessed a certain prophetic charism for the declaration of the Word of God, yet at the same time this more or less natural element—and in particular its presumptuous misuse—had already been sharply criticized by the prophets. Jeremiah had scornfully confronted the politicizing "peace priests" and "peace prophets" who were not commissioned by Yahweh (Jer 6:14; 8:11; 23:17, and so on). And even in the postexilic Psalm 85 we hear such a "cultic prophet" proclaiming his "priestly oracle of salvation". It was the magical and automatic aspect of the old cult, which seemed to dispense with an existential faith—to say nothing of the toleration of idol worship within the Temple—that the prophets attacked. And Jesus himself—who prays in the Temple and attends the liturgical feasts, who sends those he heals to the priests and even teaches men to respect the "cathedra" of the Pharisees and scribes—does not criticize the existing office or its authority as such but, rather, its abuse. He knows that only he himself can achieve the perfect identity of office and existence and that all the previous attempts can therefore only claim an anticipatory validity in reference to him (Lk 24:25ff.; Jn 5:46; 8:56). If the Letter to the Hebrews emphasizes the gulf between the earlier "mere" institution and its present fulfillment in the personal obedience of Christ, then, conversely, the image of the shepherd,[3] which Jesus takes over from the Old Covenant and applies to himself, shows the unbroken continuity between them.

God is the Shepherd of Israel (Psalm 23). In this image, as in the beginning, authority and action are perfectly identical. And starting from this origin, God establishes "shepherds" to represent him in Israel—Moses and David were true shepherds[4]—shepherds who were to pasture his flock by his commission and in his spirit. And when the shepherds start "feeding themselves" instead of the sheep and the flock goes astray in the mountains, then God

[3] On the figure of the shepherd, see bibliographies by Joachim Jeremias, article "Poimen", in *Theologisches Wörterbuch zum Neuen Testament* (1959); Odo Kiefer, *Die Hirtenrede*, Stuttgarter Biblische Studien 23 (1967); A. J. Simonis, *Die Hirtenrede im Johannisevangelium*, Analecta Biblica 29 (Rome: Pont. Biblical Inst., 1967); I. de la Potterie, *Le Bon Pasteur*, Communio II (Rome, 1969).

[4] Cf. Dominique Barthélemy, "Zwei Hirten als Entdecker Gottes", in *Gott mit seinen Ebenbild: Umrisse einer biblischen Theologie* (Einsiedeln: Johannesverlag: 1966), 133ff.; translated from the original French edition by Dom Aldhelm Dean as *God and His Image: An Outline of Biblical Theology*, rev. ed. (San Francisco: Ignatius Press, 2007).

promises (Ezek 34) to intervene himself and to "care
for" his flock, to seek out the "lost sheep" and
"bring back the strayed", to "bind up the crip-
pled" and "strengthen the weak", to "judge between
sheep and sheep, between rams and goats", and so
on. And in order to do this he will set over them
"one shepherd, my servant David" (34:23), so that
"they shall all have one shepherd" (37:24). In the
synoptic parable, Jesus describes this divine Shepherd who (in him) goes in search of the lost sheep
and brings it home. In the Johannine account of the
Good Shepherd, he shows that he himself is this
divine Shepherd by being willing to go, in obedience to and on the authority of the Father, even to
the offering up of his life for his sheep—in sharp
contrast to the hirelings, who indeed perform a
ministry of sorts among the flock but shy away from
a total commitment (Jn 10). The image of a shepherd who demonstrates his authority as the "Chief
Shepherd" (1 Pet 5:4) by dying for his sheep (and
thus seemingly abandoning them) is every bit as paradoxical as the image in Hebrews of the High Priest
who appears—living—before God "with his own
(outpoured) blood" (Heb 9:12). In essence it is the
same image and the same paradox, in fact, since on
both occasions the absolute authority derives precisely from the absolute commitment. For Jesus is

the "Good (that is, right) Shepherd" and simultaneously also the "great high priest" (Heb 4:14). Once
again it is the paradox of the words of promise, in
which Jesus appears with authority to raise up on the
last day those who eat his flesh and drink his
blood—in other words, those who confess his anni-
hilation in death, through which he is able to become
the "life of the world" (Jn 6). Such authority, given
him by the Father, seems from an earthly perspective to verge on madness, on suicide (Jn 8:22), for
it is the authority freely to "lay down" his own life
(Jn 10:18). This "madness" is transcended only when
we acknowledge, in Jesus, *the identity of authority and
mission.* To such an extent is the mission personified that ultimately it is the Father who makes the
act of offering (Jn 3:16; Rom 8:32), so that it is simply the utter freedom of the salvific action of God
that is revealed in the free consent of the Son.

Everything has become personal here; the last ves-
tige of a national or earthly institution has disap-
peared. And when Jesus now passes on the Old
Testament pastoral authority and responsibility—
perfected by him—to Peter and his "fellow elders",
it still concerns the same thing as in the Old
Covenant—the representation of God, of his authority and his commitment—but now stamped with
the personal commitment of Christ and with an

allotted portion of his own unlimited authority (Mt 28:28). In the Old Covenant, as indeed throughout the Near East, the image of the shepherd was initially used to describe the king (not the priest, inasmuch as he is seen as distinct from the king; nor, indeed, the prophet), though precisely the "good" king, conscientious and aware of his responsibility. That is why Yahweh acquired the attribute, with its irreversible intrinsic sequence: authority–commitment. As far back as the oldest part of the Ethiopian Book of Enoch (prior to 160 B.C.), the history of Israel is portrayed as that of a flock of lambs beneath the Kyrios as their shepherd. Even Moses, Samuel, and David are here depicted as "sheep". The shepherd embodies divine authority, but at the same time he always embodies Yahweh's commitment to Israel as well (chaps. 88–90).[5]

When this authority, in the New Testament, passes exclusively to the person of the Son, every other religious authority has to yield to it, and when the Son bestows authority, he does so on an exclusively personal basis. Corresponding to the pattern of life of the Son, who as the one "obedient unto death" is invested with the authority of the Father,

[5] See Simonis, *Hirtenrede*, "Henoch als Hintergrund," 161–68.

this authority is bestowed in the Christian sense
only where it encounters the total readiness to commit one's life ("Simon, do you love me more than
these?"), indeed, a readiness that goes even beyond
one's own will ("they will . . . take you where you
do not wish to go"). In his *Magna Carta* for the
clergy, Peter hands on what he himself has received,
namely, that authority should be exercised "not
under compulsion but willingly, as God would have
you do it", and, moreover, "not for sordid gain but
eagerly" and not in order to "lord it over those in
your charge", but to "be examples to the flock"
(1 Pet 5:2f.). The constantly recurring expression
used by Paul for the leadership of the community
(his own and that of his fellow workers) is *kopian*,
meaning to "wear oneself out", "exhaust oneself". And hence, precisely because this dedication
is evident to the Christian people, they are to "put
yourselves at the service" (1 Cor 16:16) of these
leaders and to "respect" them (1 Thess 5:12) and
not refuse them the fruit of their labors (cf. 2 Tim
2:6). In just the same way, Hebrews 13:7 sees
authority and life commitment as being in unity:
"Remember your leaders, those who spoke the
word of God to you"—authority and proclamation are seen as one—"consider the outcome of
their way of life, and imitate their faith."

3. Obedience and Criticism in the Church

At the beginning it was emphasized that authority in the Church can only be understood in a theocratic and Christocratic, not in a democratic, sense. This has the necessary safety device already built in: Christ has authority *insofar* as he is obedient to the Father unto death and in this obedience becomes the servant of all. How this is translated in terms of the Church can be seen in Paul, who understands himself as one of the "servants of Christ and stewards of God's mysteries", adding, "It is required of stewards that they be found trustworthy. . . . It is the Lord who judges me." He is not prepared to give an account to the community or to any other human court, and he also warns the community not to "pronounce judgment before the time [of God's judgment]" (1 Cor 4:1–5). On the other hand, he sets forth his way of life so openly that they themselves can draw the comparison between his official activity and his life. And in fact this is what they are meant to do. This comparison—in which the Corinthians are also invited to compare their own behavior with the faith they profess—will turn out to be to the advantage of the apostle and the disadvantage of the community. For "We are fools for the sake of Christ, but you are wise in Christ. We are weak, but you are strong. You are held in honor, but we in disrepute" ... "Already you have all you want! Already you have become rich! Quite apart from us you have become kings!" (1 Cor 4:10, 8). This contrast can be interpreted theologically: "So death is at work in us, but life in you" (2 Cor 4:12). In other words, the closeness of the apostle to the suffering of Christ has "earned" for the community its closeness to the Resurrection. But it can also be understood as a great danger: You democratic, mature Christians think you already live on the other side of the Cross, in an imaginary resurrection; we humiliated officebearers stand beneath the Cross. But because the Cross is and always will be the sole enduring means of access to the life of the Resurrection, Paul begins his school of faith again at chapter one: "Lest the cross of Christ be emptied of its power" (1 Cor 1:17), he has decided in Corinth "to know nothing among you except Jesus Christ, and him crucified" (1 Cor 2:2).

But do the People of God not have the right to perceive in their presbyters the unity of authority and mission, and hence also to form a critical judgment about whether and to what extent this unity is ascertainable? Have they not also—as a prerequisite for such a judgment—themselves received the Spirit of God in the charisms bestowed upon them to enable them to make such a judgment competently? Does not the picture of pastor and flock therefore fail completely here, inasmuch as it appears to reserve authority to the shepherd alone and only obedience to the flock? But precisely this appearance has been dispelled since Christ's obedience unto death. And here Paul steps in to resolve the seemingly confusing—not to say inextricable—dialectic of obedience and criticism in the Church. Criticism, which is by no means rejected a priori as unfitting, has one essential precondition: that those criticizing must examine themselves as to whether they "are living in the faith", must "test" themselves to see whether "Jesus Christ is in you" (2 Cor 13:5). Needless to say, this means the Jesus Christ whose mystery of obedience unto death is and always will be the precondition for his resurrected "pneumatic" (spirit-filled) existence. Were those who criticize not to submit themselves to such an examination, then they would have failed to "meet the test". They would not be standing at the center of Christian existence—from which position alone it is possible to evaluate the Christian existence of an officebearer. Paul, however, hopes that "you will find out that *we* have not failed"—and precisely because he is configured in his own life to Christ and to the pattern of his authority.

"For he was crucified in weakness, but lives by the power of God. For we are weak in him, but in dealing with you we will live with him by the power of God" (13:4). Thus he is hoping that the Corinthians will understand the paradox of authority within the Church by experiencing in faith the mystery of Christ, ("when I am weak, then I am strong" 12:10). And once again he is ready to allow them the flattering role of maturity, while taking upon himself the vicarious humiliation: "But we pray God that you may not do wrong—not that *we* may appear to have met the test, but that *you* may do what is right, though we may seem to have failed.... For we are glad when we are weak and you are strong." For the entire authority of the New Testament officebearer has its meaning solely in the building up of the community. Here again the contrast appears between "fleshly" authority in the Old Covenant and "spiritual" authority in the New. Whereas Jeremiah is given the power "to pluck up and to break down, to destroy and to overthrow, to build and to plant" (Jer 1:10), Paul says—obviously with this in mind—"I write this while I am away from you, in order that when I come I may not have to be severe in my use of the authority which the Lord has given me for building up and not for tearing down" (2 Cor 13:10).

Earlier, it is true, he has said that "the weapons of our warfare are not worldly but have divine (spiritual) power to destroy strongholds. We destroy arguments and every proud obstacle to the knowledge of God" (2 Cor 10:4f.). But then again he shows that he wishes to exercise this power always and only in agreement with the believing, understanding, consenting community. So it is with the exclusion of the man who has committed incest. Paul has indeed already pronounced judgment himself, but he wishes to implement it together with the community gathered around him in the Spirit (1 Cor 5:3ff.). And he is "ready to punish every disobedience, when your obedience is complete", so that this obedience can concur in the justice of this punishment (2 Cor 10:6). He can threaten the use of a "naked" exercise of authority if he sees that the community, in its criticism of authority, is in danger of falling away from the ecclesial *communio* of faithful and loving obedience. But as a man of the Church, he understands such a situation as a fundamentally impossible extreme case that would signify a fiasco, a failure of the Church, for it would make manifest the rupture of that *communio* which, according to Paul, acquires its inner form essentially through an office lived and exercised in conformity to Christ. "For I fear that perhaps *I* may come and find *you* not what

I wish, and that *you* may find *me* not what *you* wish; that perhaps there may be quarreling, jealousy, anger, selfishness, slander, gossip, conceit, and disorder. I fear that when I come again my God may humble me before you.... If I come again I will not spare them—since you desire proof that Christ is speaking in me" (2 Cor 12:20f.; 13:2f.). To the extent that this proof is demanded in a spirit of "putting (God) to the test", a spirit of "contestation" (as with Massah and Meribah, Ex 17:7), it cannot be supplied by the authority in the manner envisaged by the Church but only in the disguised and humiliating form of *absolute* power. But then the community would be to blame for this in having failed to meet the test.

This is not to say that the community cannot or should not exercise any critical function with regard to authority. Since the leaders of the communities are supposed "to equip the saints for the work of ministry" (Eph 4:12ff.) and lead them out of a condition of immaturity, in both faith and life, and educate them to "speak the truth in love" (cf. Eph 4:12ff.) and since, with the help of this education toward fully responsible action, every member—the whole body—is "joined and knit together" in reciprocal service, there undoubtedly exists an exchange between the Christians and their leaders. Indeed, Paul himself always wants to be built up, consoled, spiritually accompanied, and encouraged by the communities. The *paraclesis*—both as consolation and as admonitory cautioning—runs back and forth in an interplay between all the members of the Body of Christ. In this way the positive contribution of every member of the community—which can and must also be a critical contribution—is brought in for the building up of the whole. That priests can go astray, that criticisms may be leveled at them from within the community and that they may have to be rebuked by the bishop "in the presence of all"—albeit "without favor" and not "from partiality"—is something already foreseen in the pastoral epistles (1 Tim 5:20f.). Among other things, the leader must also be "gentle" (3:3) toward these men. But it is always expected (as a minimum standard) that he be "an example in speech and conduct, in love, in faith, in purity" (1 Tim 4:12)—just as Paul understood himself to be an example (*typos*) who for his part has been marked by Christ. With this proviso, Paul encourages his successor in a sort of holy steadfastness that from the outside might look like rigidity, but which from within is nothing other than the obedience and responsibility of the officebearer toward his Lord.

We do not need to follow all the meanderings of Paul's self-defense vis-à-vis the community. Nor do we need to present it as a concrete model for every detail of subsequent disputes within the Church. The essential thing about it—drawn out as it is over several chapters of one of Paul's principal epistles—is the simple fact that we are actually given an example here of the dialogue between ecclesial office and contesting community. It would be unreasonable to assert that this dialogue was of merely historical interest because in later times no bishop or priest could claim to have the same authority as an apostle. There are no such antiquities in the New Testament. The practical doctrinal teaching of the two letters to the Corinthians has the same scope as the soteriology of Romans and Galatians. It should have been taken just as seriously by Protestant theology as these were. For it translates the doctrine of salvation into the present day of the Church, a Church that still possesses the same fundamental structure with which she began in the apostolic age.

Paul argues on the basis of his own life, which is essentially congruent with his office yet about which he will boast only insofar as it has been conformed, by the grace of God, to the Lord. Not many officebearers in the later Church are able—or willing—to follow him in such an exhibition of his existence (in "foolishness"). Yet all of them will have Paul's example before their mind's eye—particularly since he in his desire to use "naked" authority only in an extreme case and in his efforts to do everything in order to prevent such a case and, with the mind of Christ, to overcome the difference between office and community. Not least in that he makes the judging and contesting community to reflect in its judgment of the frailties of those in office.

ON THE PRIESTLY MINISTRY

In an article such as this there is space to say only a little. Many important aspects will not be taken into consideration, so that we can focus on one central point alone, which because of urgent pastoral-psychological pressure and sociological needs as well as dialogical-ecumenical concerns, has almost been forgotten and yet is theologically central. Let us leave behind us all the paternalism of earlier cultural stages—all the mysticism of representation that is associated with eras characterized by symbolic thinking or supported by a baroque theology of enlightenment and, finally, all the juridicism of the recent teaching on the *sacra potestas*—as relativistic and let us focus on the simple truth: to be a Christian in the first place—and hence also to be a priest—is to imitate the Redeemer who came to serve, the Servant of Yahweh who in washing the disciples' feet gave us the example of what we also are to do for one another.

This is the great "discovery" of Vatican II, and everyone agrees on this. But not equally when it

comes to imitating him in that ministry which is
the distinctive ministry of Christ: the Mount of
Olives, the Cross. Being serious about the washing of the feet, which is taking upon oneself, in
humiliation, the dirt of one's brethren. This is the
priesthood of the New Testament; not the contin-
uation of the Aaronic priesthood in which only the
blood of animals was shed, but rather the crowning of those mysterious anticipatory episodes where
one man stepped forward for a sinful people, under
the lightning flash of God's wrath: Abraham, the
Moses of Deuteronomy, Jeremiah, Ezekiel, Job, the
deuterocanonical Isaiah. The Letter to the Hebrews,
which emphasizes the rupture with the Aaronic
priesthood, is well aware of this continuity with the
great examples of renunciation and sacrifice and
urges Christians to follow the greatest of those sac-
rificed, the archetype and leader (*Archegos*), "outside the camp" and to the Cross. With Paul, this
following into shared suffering with Christ—for the
brethren, for the community, as well as for the Jew-
ish brethren who stood apart—becomes evident. By
no means merely (in the Protestant sense) as a sign
pointing to the sole Mediator (*apart* from whom
there can be no other—which is true—yet one can
be *in* Him: *en* Christo) and by no means merely as
a kind of "witness function", unless it be as

martyrion, with one's life: "I have been crucified with Christ" [Gal 2:20].

The Twelve, who will later take over the office of leadership, are first given training in the existential following to the Cross. "Are you able to drink the cup that I am to drink? ... You will drink my cup ..." (Mt 20:22f.). "You are those who have stayed with me in my trials" (Lk 22:28).

Christ's public years, his service as the Word of God, are to a great extent the conclusion, the transcendent synthesis of the Old Testament prophetic word. The New Covenant is actually established only with the slaughter of the new *Pascha*—in the night of the Cross. It is here, for the first time in fact, that the most intimate aspect of God's love is revealed—the Trinity. Revealed in the harrowing opposition between "Father, all things are possible to you" and "but what you will" (Mk 14:36); between the "worm", "scorned by men", and the veiled, absent, averted face of God. No "dialogical situation" now, but the absolute obedience of a pure servant toward the Love that has veiled itself as pure Authority. The love of God goes much farther—for our sakes—than our lukewarmness and sinfulness are able to conceive as love.

It is precisely here, in the night of the Cross, that the New Testament priestly office originates. At the point where the full gravity of the New Testament emerges in the first place—beyond the limits of our own willing, our understanding, even our capacity for doing (for it is only the one who "can do no more" who truly suffers). Clearly, to arrive at this place is possible only for the one who truly loves, who has already spent long years engaged with God in prayer, in a dialogue of love. Even for the Son of God, the "official" face of the Father is no more than the final phase, the ultimate venture in a perpetual dialogue of love, of a reciprocity, in the breath of the Holy Spirit, without which the work of redemption could never have succeeded. We recognize this reciprocity of loving service also in the Church of Christ, where to "preside"—and thus to command—never departs from the law that all the members are to "serve one another" in love (Gal 5:13) and be "subject" to one another. The service of official command is in no sense excluded by this law; rather it is expressly rooted in it, in contrast to worldly authority, which must necessarily prevail even over the unwilling by force of compulsion (Mt 20:25ff.).

The last Council rightly emphasized—against a somewhat precipitate structural equation of temporal and ecclesial law—the loving and ministering *togetherness* between the member of Christ who commands and the member who obeys, the dialogical situation between the two, and the Christian responsibility of the one who commands.

But following Christ nonetheless requires ecclesial obedience toward ecclesial office to be ready to follow the Lord even to the ultimate situation, which truly brings salvation and is at the same time the acid test for the individual of his *real* willingness to obey—to obey the other and not simply himself, his own good will, his good intentions and ideal agenda. Only on the Mount of Olives—in the greatest *diastasis* and contrast between Father and Son, between the One who inexorably commands and the One who is obedient beyond human strength, in which the Spirit appears as the "rule" of the Father and as the "willing beyond willing" of the Son—only here is the Trinity truly revealed. Here, where the love of God for sinners assumes the aspect of purely official authority—and indeed necessarily so, according to the plan of salvation, since the world is redeemed not through "freedom" and "maturity" but by being "obedient unto death, even (the most shameful) death". It is from here that the innermost structure of the Church must originate. Otherwise, her members would never ever be in the place where the principal event is happening. Otherwise Mary would not have to stand beneath the Cross and be abandoned by her Son ("behold your other son");

otherwise Christian love would never get farther
than ethics and humanism, in which the (conscientious!) individual still retains the measure and the
initiative in hand. The Son in suffering must take
upon himself the final humiliation in place of sinners; and the Father, out of love for the world and
for the Son, takes on the (terrible!) office of humbling him. When Peter is finally installed in office,
he is first of all humbled (by the threefold question) and then given the promise that he will follow to the Cross—in other words, in suffering
beyond his own willing: "Another will gird you and
carry you where you do not wish to go" [Jn 21:18].
It is at this price that he can and must exercise the
humiliating office of humbling his brethren (in
shared obedience to Christ, Heb 5:9), humbling
them toward God. The situation *kat exochen* in
which this happens is the confessional. Of course,
the ministry of the Cross is tempered here by Resurrection love; yet, nonetheless, the confessional is
no "dialogue situation" but the place where the sinner submits to the judgment of the office that—
according to the norm of Christ and with the power
of heaven—binds or loses. Naturally, all Christian
obedience toward the Mother Church, all priestly
obedience toward governing authority, derives theologically from here, from the Cross, and cannot

otherwise be justified. In order to be able to ask this of his own, Christ himself "offered up prayers and supplications, with loud cries and tears" to the Father, who "was able to save him from death ... for his godly fear" [1] and "although he was a Son, he learned obedience through what he suffered" (Heb 5:7f.).

Fundamentally, every Christian must be prepared for this obedience, which is a true dying with Christ (our Baptism contains this grace and this requirement!). It is however clear that anyone in the Church chosen for the humiliation of having to command officially must die to himself in a particularly radical manner. For how else could he, as a sinner, escape the dangers of confusing spiritual with temporal power, of reinforcing the former with the latter, of "representing", of abusing this authority? So it is that the call for renunciation in the Sermon on the Mount, while addressed to all, is spoken with "his eyes on his disciples" (Lk 6:20), and we are even told that "he taught them" (Mt 5:2). The call to leave everything in order to risk everything on the one card that is Christ and to follow him alone is indeed addressed to all (Lk 14:25), yet it is

[1] The meaning of this verse is disputed. See C. Spicq, *Lettre aux Hebreux II* (1953), 114–17. However, this in no way changes the over-all meaning.

followed quite literally by subsequent officebearers (Mt 19:27). This "leaving everything" is the characteristic sign of witness that distinguishes the Christian in general but, far more clearly still, the officebearers as well—a sign that is further greatly reinforced by celibacy. For marriage, as a natural institution, is not as such a witness to Christ, whereas celibacy "for the sake of the kingdom of heaven" [Mt 19:12] is indeed so, in the highest measure—and particularly so, in fact, in the sense of the humiliation in the face of an uncomprehending, scandalized world.

In the New Covenant there can be no "office" that is not existentially "covered"—since Christ is indeed both Priest and Victim—and therefore whoever has the ministry of providing the divine-official function for the benefit of the community must himself bear witness that he is one who renounces out of love and is "bound" (cf. Jn 21:18) beyond what he himself wishes. Out of love. Just as ultimately—seemingly contrary to all the logic of John's Gospel, in which after all Peter embodies the "office" and John the "love" (clearly so in 20:1–10)—all "love" has to be contained in the official Peter ("do you love me more than these?" 21:15). Hence it will not do to "sociologize" the New Testament office, to regard it as a mere "function" within the community of the "People of God" and to assign it any form of life (marriage, celibacy) as though it were conducted in an entirely neutral way in this regard. Through this kind of "sociologizing", it becomes "de-theologized", detached from the existential event of the Cross—for its "dignity" consists in the grace of humiliation together with the suffering Lord—it becomes something banal and loses its power to attract the generous-hearted.

That it is a humbling thing to command officially, and that this humiliation must be experienced, understood, borne—in other words, that human helplessness and ecclesial authority interact together in the most paradoxical way, which can only be accepted by a living faith—is something that could be clearly demonstrated by a close analysis of Paul's discourse on "foolishness" in 2 Corinthians about theory and practice. This letter remains the Magna Carta of New Testament priestly ministry in its unbroken, undiluted paradox of the Cross.

One final thing: How could the Christian people have the *sensus fidei* if they did not know or sense these things (often better than the clergy)? Even putting aside all popular superstition (in a certain kind of magical priestly power), there still remains a solid and healthy core of Christian popular instinct. People want and seek priests who are humble, who truly pray and are close to God. Wherever such a priest is found (and many travel far and wide to find him, as a confessor, for instance), people *want* to obey spiritually when commanded spiritually through this office. Anyone who undermines this *sensus fidei* in the laity is a gravedigger of the Catholic Church, as is anyone who seeks to blunt the existential scandal of the priestly existence by invoking sociological considerations. The ministry of Christ is no ordinary form of social service: "The Son of man came not to be served but to serve, *and* to give his life as a ransom for many" (Mt 20:28). All of this is wholly independent of any restructuring of modern society. Of course, there are many time-conditioned and often undesirable links between ecclesial office and outmoded social structures that need to be broken. And as a result, the priestly ministry may perhaps emerge into a new and very Christian vulnerability, once the protective shell of feudal and juridical paternalism has fallen away. Then how unprotected the "paternalism of the Mount of Olives" will stand! Yet it is this alone that counts. It is service, nothing but service. But a heavy service, since it must be able, in the name of the God on the Cross, to command divinely, too.

MINISTERIAL PRIESTHOOD AND
THE PEOPLE OF GOD

Social restructuring that calls into question the idea of a priestly state, misunderstandings and misuse of spiritual authority at all levels of Church leadership, ecumenical considerations, and finally, the general trend toward challenging every form of institutional authority have brought profound unease to the heart of the Catholic Church. Is her ministerial priesthood accounted for at all sufficiently by its New Testament foundations, or is it merely a structure only fully established in the post-apostolic era (around A.D. 100, though seen already in Titus 1:5) and in given circumstances to be dismantled again?

As we know from the Letter to the Hebrews, Jesus is the superlative fulfillment of the Old Covenant Aaronic priesthood—according to which he himself is not a priest at all (Heb 7:11f.)—and hence, from Jesus' self-consecration and self-sacrifice for the world, every Christian within the Church is marked with the stamp of priesthood by virtue of his Baptism. Thus the "head and body" of Christ together henceforth seem to form a single, indivisible priesthood, and the "community leaders" mentioned in the New Testament merely possess a "charism", one ministry among others, which in given circumstances can be entrusted to them and taken away again by the Church (or community).

True though it is that there is no direct line leading from the Old Covenant to the New Covenant priesthood, the view just outlined is one-sided nevertheless. It fails to take into account some essential facts of the New Testament—just three of which are to be very briefly mentioned here. These three arguments in no way call into question the general priesthood of the Church—which is, however, oddly enough justified in 1 Peter 2:5, 9 with an Old Covenant quotation: Exodus 19:6! The existence of a ministerial priesthood within the People of God should be founded neither on a "generally religious" nor on an "overall biblical" basis but, instead, on a specifically christological and ecclesial one.

1. *In many places in the Synoptic Gospels the apostles are chosen by Jesus as his companions, given special authority (exousia), and sent out (Mk 3:14).* And this mission consists in more than merely preaching: "Preach as you go, saying, 'The kingdom of heaven is at hand.' Heal the sick, raise the dead, cleanse lepers, cast out demons" (Mt 10:7f.). The deeds they

are given authority to perform are the proof that the Kingdom of heaven is a present power, a power that has Jesus as its center; indeed, it is he himself who performs all these deeds with the "authority" that is his own (Mk 1:22, 27). The miraculous signs that "prove" that the Messiah has come (Mt 11:4f.) are the provisional, sensory form, appropriate to the mortal life of Jesus, the illustration of his ultimate authority to lay down his life for the world and to receive it back again in the Resurrection—for himself and for distribution to all (Jn 10:18). Therefore it is logical that those who before his death were authorized with the powers of the coming Kingdom of God on earth should after Christ's death and Resurrection likewise retain the authority over the now-achieved fullness of the Kingdom (that is centrally Jesus himself)—and indeed in the same oppositional relationship to the People of God as in the first mission. One need only observe the behavior of the apostles in the Acts of the Apostles— and in particular the behavior of Paul toward his communities—to see how powerfully the apostles are aware of their authority, both as duty and as burden. The image of the apostle (for example, in the letters to the Corinthians) corresponds in all its basic outlines precisely to that of the disciples sent out in Matthew 10, even though the text of Matthew 10 can in no sense be described as dependent on Paul. And even if, at every level of the New Testament, the one authorized by God and Christ is exhorted to the humility of service—indeed, to the "lowest place"—his authority is never thereby called into question; rather, the attitude is indicated in which alone it may be exercised. It is just as evident at every level that what is involved, both in the pre-Paschal as in the post-Paschal authorization and mission, is not a transitory but rather an enduring structure of the People of God (see for example Eph 4:11, where the commissioned "pastors", "teachers", and so on, are called to "build up" the Christian people for the exercise of their Christian mission in the world).

2. *This is made evident in the biblical image of the shepherd*. In the writings of the prophets (especially Ezekiel 34), God thrusts aside the undutiful shepherds of his people and promises to take over himself the task of pasturing his sheep. This function requires that he assume ownership of the flock, know his animals individually, examine them, count them, "review" them (34:12), "judge" between weak and strong animals, carry the weak "in his bosom" (Is 40:11), and lead them all into "green pastures" (Ps 23), and so forth. God promises that he will in the end send a true shepherd of Israel, yet in the Old Covenant he has already chosen two great shepherds—Moses, who

tends Jethro's sheep, and David, who while still a
shepherd boy is anointed king. For both of them,
the office of shepherd becomes just a succession of
difficulties. Increasingly, they come to suffer for the
people, and this role is continued by the prophets
until it receives, in the image of the "suffering servant", its highest and purest form. Jesus is the perfection of these lines. In the parable of the lost sheep,
he reveals the mind of the Father (as in Ezekiel 34)
but at the same time his own mind (cf. Mt 9:36);
and John (chap. 10) describes him as the Good
Shepherd, who (as the Servant) lays down his life
for his sheep. The shepherd who sheds his blood for
the flock is at the same time the Lamb slaughtered
for all. Now the issue of ministerial "authority" in
living communion with Jesus receives a new illu-
mination: for whoever is given the sheep of Jesus to
pasture (Jn 21:15–17) must at the same time be
ready to let himself be led where he "does not wish
to go"—in the sacrifice and death on the Cross
(Jn 21:18–19). Paul shows—precisely at the point
where he needs sacerdotal expressions for his apostolic ministry—the inseparability of ministry and life
commitment (self-sacrifice) (see Rom 15:16; 1:9;
Phil 2:17; 2 Tim 4:6). Wherever a Christian pastor
performs official actions without offering himself
unreservedly for the flock, violence is done to the

Christian life. Even if one cannot say that such priestly actions are simply invalid—that would be heretical—yet one must still say—since in Christ office and life have become identical—that for a Christian officebearer the highest possible degree of convergence is not merely appropriate but an absolute requirement. This is where the theological justification for celibacy needs to be applied (that shepherd who goes in search of the lost sheep, persevering "until he finds it" [Lk 15:4], cannot break off his search because more urgent duties call him home to wife and child).

3. If Christ, in a Christianity that is liberated from the Law and called to the freedom of the children of God, nevertheless establishes authority—and how Paul insists on this authority from Christ in regard to the community—then it is *Because he has redeemed the world from the disobedience of sin through his obedience to the Father.*

Here ecclesial obedience moves into the field of christological and trinitarian Mystery and thus escapes the ultimate competence of any sociological or organizational perspective. If the redemption occurs through an absolute obedience of Jesus to the will and "commandment" (*mandatum*) of the Father, then two inseparable mysteries of the faith are in this obedience. On the one hand, there is the original mutual understanding of the Son with the Father, in the shared Holy Spirit—the one and only divine Will for the redemption of the world, as made known in the entire life of Jesus right up to the Passion (cf. the temptation account or such passages as John 4:34: "My food is to do the will of him who sent me and to accomplish his work"). On the other hand, there is the opposition on the Mount of Olives: "Not my will, but yours, be done". Humanly speaking, one could say that in eternity Father and Son were (or are) united in agreement that their common work will have to go to the point of the most painful opposition. The Church participates in this mystery, to a degree that would have to be exactly determined (but for which there is insufficient space here). Between the ministerial priesthood and the community there exists a presumptive unity—that the will of the triune God might be done, that Christ might truly "live in me", as hard as it may be for me to deny myself and go beyond myself into the will of Christ. There is a heavy and burdensome ministry that demands, with authority from above, this self-mastery so painful to the sinner—yet which as one who is baptized he still fundamentally desires. It is genuine authority, not merely a reference to the unique authority of Christ, for "He who hears you hears me." And yet it is only genuine authority when it is really required in the name of and by the authority of Christ—and for this difficult differentiation due consideration must be given to the right of the People of God to be heard, the moment of "the immediacy of God" for every Christian conscience. Paul shows that he never exercises authority in the abstract or in isolation but always presumes and seeks the original spirit of mutual agreement with the community and appeals to it (cf. 2 Cor 13:3–10, for example). But that is another problem—between the authoritarian and the "democratic" moments in the Church. Our concern here was merely to demonstrate the existence of priestly authority as such in the New Covenant.

SOURCES

The publication of this book was prompted by a footnote by Hans Urs von Balthasar in *Unser Auftrag* (*Our Task*), where he cited the following works on the priestly ministry:

On Priestly Spirituality

"Über priesterliche Spiritualität", *Kontact: Zeitschrift der Theologen des Collegium Borromaeum*, no. 14 (Freiburg im Breislau), 4–14.

Mary and the Office of the Priest

"Maria und das Priesteramt". Printed manuscript. Lecture of September 11, 1978. Published by the Marianischen Priesterkongregation of the Diocese of Augsburg. 16p.

The Priest I Seek

"Der Priester, den ich suche". In *Klarstellungen: Zur Prüfung der Geister*, 99–106. Einsiedeln: Johannes

Verlag, 1971; 4th ed., 1978. Translated by John Riches as "The Priest I Want", in *Elucidations*, 161–72 (San Francisco: Ignatius Press, 1998). Newly translated here.

Office and Existence

"Amt und Existenz". From: *Die Wahrheit ist symphonisch*, 116–30. Einsiedeln, 1972. Translated by Graham Harrison as "Office and Existence", in *Truth Is Symphonic* (San Francisco: Ignatius Press, 1987). Newly translated here.

On the Priestly Ministry

"Über das priesterliche Amt". *Civitas: Monatsschrift des Schweiz. Studentenvereins* 23 (Lucerne, July 1968): 794–97.

Ministerial Priesthood and the People of God

"Amtspriestertum und Gottesvolk". In *Pfarrblatt Katholisch Basel* 56, no. 39 (September 26, 1969).